'Was it something I said?'

Ali Yassine

'Was it something I said?'

the voice of
Cardiff City

First impression: 2011

© Ali Yassine & Y Lolfa Cyf., 2011

The publishers wish to acknowledge the support of
Cyngor Llyfrau Cymru

Cover design: Y Lolfa
Cover photograph: Peter Thomas

ISBN: 978 1 84771 233 2

FSC

Published and printed in Wales
on paper from well maintained forests by
Y Lolfa Cyf., Talybont, Ceredigion SY24 5HE
e-mail ylolfa@ylolfa.com
website www.ylolfa.com
tel 01970 832 304
fax 832 782

CHAPTER 1

It started with a kiss.

A kiss of death, that is, for Bobby Gould's career as Cardiff City's manager, after just one season in charge. That event, and the fact that as a freelancer in broadcasting, I was what is commonly known in media circles as 'resting' or, to put it bluntly, unemployed, prompted me to throw my hat in the ring for the vacant manager's position.

And, after a few, long, angst-ridden minutes working out the best way to highlight my somewhat limited footballing credentials – the following was the resulting letter of application:

> *Your Excellency, Sam bin Hammam bin Wimbledon,*
>
> *I am writing to you to apply for the role of manager of Cardiff City Football Club. Indeed, having no experience and little knowledge of running either a competitive football team (or any other sporting team, for that matter), nor the ability to motivate, deal in the transfer market or make crucial tactical decisions, I feel that I am the ideal candidate for the job.*
>
> *However, I'm not bad on FIFA manager and can do four keepy-uppies if it's not too windy. I also have some great ideas to improve team morale and to ensure that Cardiff City become a team of champions.*
>
> *My first suggestion is stamp a Welsh identity on all the players by changing their names to Jones. This would also help to confuse the opposition and referee, whilst also making communication with the team during matches and training sessions far simpler. All I'd have to do to get my points across is to shout, "Oi, Jonesy, pass*

*the ball to Jonesy!" or, "Keep it tight, Jonesy!" or indeed, in
the unlikely event of seeing one of our players in the box, "Shoot
Jonesy!" Granted, it might also confuse our own players to have
the same name but having spent years watching them in the lower
divisions, this might not be such a bad thing. In fact, I'm confident
that it could help improve them. I'm also prepared to change my own
name to Jones and to employ a backroom staff of Joneses.*

*Among other ideas, I would like to change the club's cuisine to
offer a range of my mum's Egyptian curries as well as balti, sushi
and vegan dishes, change the club's mascot to an Ayatollah and to
introduce a karaoke half-time show with your good self in the lead
role under the title 'Sing along a Sam'.*

*Despite a seeming lack of experience in football, I can assure
you that I have an extensive background in logistics and man
management, and am more than capable of coping with extreme
pressure in a work environment. Indeed, for proof of this, please
do not hesitate to contact my previous employer, Pizza Express in
Caerphilly.*

At the end of the letter, I suggested that if my
qualifications were deemed unsuitable, I would be available
as a bilingual tannoy announcer.

★

In hindsight, I suppose the main reason for sending the letter
was to get a reply on Cardiff City headed notepaper with a
'thanks, but no thanks' for my application. Indeed, the whole
point had been to produce a rejection in order to prove to
the Unemployment Benefit Office that I was actively seeking
employment. Imagine my shock then a week later, when I
received a telephone call asking me to attend a meeting at

Ninian Park. "Yeah… um… sure," I mumbled, stunned by the request. Having quickly jotted a date and time, I put the receiver down completely baffled. Thoughts started racing through my head. They weren't that desperate for a manager, surely!

Thankfully, they weren't. Julian Jenkins, the club's head of media, wanted to chat about my interest in becoming the club's tannoy announcer. As luck would have it, the then 'voice of the Bluebirds' Phil Suarez, a man that had done everything at Cardiff City, from driving the team bus and organising fundraisers to conducting live radio interviews and writing match reports, was moving on to a new role of internet commentator. This meant that the position of tannoy announcer had recently become available. Julian wanted to see how I'd perform on the microphone. "Now?" I asked when prompted to speak to an empty Ninian Park. "Yes, now," he replied. At the time, I had just finished working as a radio presenter for BBC Radio Cymru and had also recently finished acting on S4C's hospital drama, *Glan Hafren* – a sort of Welsh language version of *Casualty*. Performing, therefore, was nothing new and, after a short audition in front of Julian, a few disinterested ground staff and a couple of passing seagulls, I was offered the job. Never in a million years had I ever thought that I'd get to work for my favourite football team, let alone still be there ten years later. Also, considering most managers rarely last a few seasons, the tannoy wasn't such a bad option after all.

CHAPTER 2

I was ten years old when I made my first trip to Ninian Park – having had free tickets from school – mainly on account that nobody else wanted them. The tickets were for a Wales under-18 game against England and as I left our terraced house in the heart of Cardiff Docks, I can still remember the worried look on my mother's face, not quite sure why she was letting me go. In those days, the early 1970s, it wasn't unusual for youngsters to go wandering off, finding their feet in the big wide world, and I was as keen to get out and about as any of my peers. At least my mother knew I'd be home when the game finished, or earlier, if I got hungry. However, unbeknown to me at the time, racism was rife outside of our cocooned little community, and parents such as mine did their best to shelter their kids from the brunt of it. In saying that, I was one of life's daydreamers and way too naive to have known if people were being racist or not, always innocently looking for the best, rather than worst, in people.

I walked to the ground that day with a school pal, Paul Skagestad, the son of a Norwegian dockworker. In fact, our mutual love of the beautiful game has kept our friendship strong to this very day. We still watch matches together, mainly televised City away games but also the odd away trip or pre-season friendly. And we still react in the same crazy, ecstatic way every time City score.

Anyway, we got to the ground quite early to savour the atmosphere and, after squeezing through the narrow turnstiles, planted ourselves at the front of the Canton

Stand. In its latter days the Canton Stand became the Spar Family Stand but, back then, it was certainly not a place for families nor, it has to be said, the faint-hearted. With its long wooden benches full to the brim with mainly working-class men swigging on bottles of brown ale, puffing away on Park Drive cigarettes and cussing to their hearts delight, the Canton Stand was an intimidating place, especially for a couple of ten year olds. In fact, I remember surveying the scene around me with awe and felt quite grown up by the end of the game having survived its intensity and, much to my parent's disgust, having also picked up a whole new vocabulary.

The cussing, it has to be said, had been totally justified. Wales had lost, again! Quite convincingly as it happens. In all honesty, however, it came as no surprise to me. Even at the tender age of ten, I had an inkling that my parents had settled in a country that wasn't known for its footballing prowess. Mind you, living within a short distance of the world-famous Arms Park and watching my hometown being taken over every year by legions of rugby fans from all over Principality kind of gave me a big clue as to where sporting priorities lay in Wales. Yet, despite having nothing against rugby, watching my favourite pastime reduced to a second-class status made me love football even more. I simply couldn't get enough of it: from the meagre rations of televised football in the 1960s and 1970s to the local park fixtures. Indeed, after my first Ninian Park experience, I was determined to watch more live football, especially Cardiff City games, and with little or, to be perfectly honest, no funds whatsoever, gaining entry to the ground became a regular challenge.

Over the course of the next few years, and with the help of other football-mad but equally broke youngsters, I learned almost every trick available of how to get into Ninian Park without paying, from circumnavigating the railway tracks and sneaking under the corrugated sheets of metal that surrounded the back of the Bob Bank to persuading a turnstile operator to turn a blind eye.

It has to be said that the old-style terracing was a great help in my endeavour to watch the Bluebirds. Indeed, many of us used to hang around the exit gates for any opportunity to get into the ground. The ability to blend in with others meant that youngsters like me, given the slightest chance of entry, could try rushing in en masse knowing that, despite the likelihood of at least one or two getting caught, a good many of us would get in to satisfy our footballing fix. In my case, being black was a bit of a hindrance. I stood out like a sore thumb. However, I soon learned that by sitting on a terrace until kick-off time, surrounded by standing adults until the area became full, detection was very unlikely. Also, with the help of a carefully placed ladder, thanks to a school friend whose garden backed onto the Grange End, entry could be made with relative ease.

I also took in as many free games as I could, such as City's reserve team fixtures or, when desperate to get a fix, watching their training sessions, which took place a couple of hundred yards from Ninian Park on a pitch located next to the city's bus depot.

Later, it became apparent to many of us that we could watch football and make money. As with many grounds, much of Ninian Park was made of wood, particularly the

Grange End. Whenever the team scored, celebrating fans would jump up and down, shaking the stand to its core, often dropping coins in the large gaps underfoot. Many of us would then rush underneath the stand to collect any loose change that had fallen through the gaps above. Lads from different areas of Cardiff used to battle it out to have the right to control the flow of money that fell. However, one of the pitfalls of such an endeavour was the trickle of urine that sometimes accompanied the trickle of money – the result of fans that couldn't be bothered going to one of the open toilets behind the Grange End, preferring instead to relieve themselves where they stood. In fact, it became a kind of initiation to have been soaked by an anonymous pisser, with many of us egging on unsuspecting newcomers by claiming it was merely a leaking tap, and howling in laughter when a chosen victim, often from a rival area in Cardiff, realised that his damp clothes stank to high heaven of human liquid waste.

Looking back, it's incredible to think how much the experience of going to a football match has changed since my first visit to Ninian Park – especially for children. I guess one of the main changes has been the increase in the number of women who now attend matches with their children, boys and girls, compared to the 1970s when it was just young boys with their dads. It's fair to say that hardly any women ever went in my early years at Ninian Park, other than the few ladies that worked in the food kiosks or were members of the St John's Ambulance Brigade, and those had to have skins as thick as rhinos to deal with the banter thrown at them. Facilities too, of course, are so much better these days. Cardiff City's new stadium has an amazing family stand with PlayStations on the concourses and large television screens playing the latest cartoons. Kids also now have a vast array of merchandising available to them, from replica shirts and fashion wear to books, DVDs and computer accessories. All I could remember being on sale during my childhood was the basic, but compulsory, blue and white scarf or bobble hat, and a folder to keep programmes in.

That said, it was the football that appealed to my peers and me more than any merchandise available or the type of facilities on offer. It had an edge about it back then, a welcome release from the drudgery of an eight-hour shift for the working classes and, for us kids, a break from the monotony of school. Corporate hospitality, if it existed back then, was certainly not an option to most and a pre-match meal, if you were flush, was a steaming hot pie and an equally steaming hot Bovril, so hot that it burned the inside of your mouth and almost every organ as it passed through your system. Footballers were different too. Indeed, other than the very big names, players were unlikely to be seen driving top of the range sports cars. Most were still part of their local communities, often travelling on public transport or drinking in their local pubs and living in the areas that nurtured their talents. A lot of them became pub landlords on retirement from the game or used their savings to start local businesses. In fact, one of those, a former Bluebirds winger, Gil Reece, was to become my landlord during my twenties, when I rented a small flat from him in Splott.

As for early heroes, I can't remember that many. I was too young to remember John Toshack or Alan Warboys playing for the club. Indeed, I may well have watched them play. Nevertheless, it's not something I can say with any degree of certainty. However, I can say that I watched Clive Charles and Derek Showers play. I remember Clive because he was the first black player I saw in a Bluebirds shirt and Derek was, and still is, the only white footballer I've ever seen with what sometimes looked, depending on how he styled it, like he had a ginger afro. In my eyes, that afro made him as good as black to me and, therefore, spiritually, a brother.

As for my early games, I guess the one memory that sticks out most was an FA Cup run in 1977 when the club reached the fifth or sixth round, knocking out Tottenham and Wrexham along the way, only to come unstuck against an Everton team that included one of British football's big stars, Duncan Mackenzie, and a certain Dave Jones. That FA Cup run also provided me with my early heroes: Tony Evans, Phil Dwyer, Peter Sayer, David Giles and John Buchanan.

I wasn't one for collecting match programmes nor did I have any interest in stats. We lost a lot, I know that, and we constantly yo-yoed between the divisions. Despite this, I look back with affection at my early years as a Cardiff City fan. Putting aside the fact that hooligans ran amok on a regular basis, that the ground was intimidating at the best of times, and that the football and food on offer were often awful, I loved it all the same.

CHAPTER 3

My first game as Cardiff City's official tannoy announcer was a pre-season friendly against Crystal Palace. Indeed, despite usually having the memory of a goldfish, particularly with regard to a lot of Bluebirds fixtures, the Palace game is one I will never forget; mostly on account of the many gaffes I made.

The day had started badly when I fell out with one of the stewards for having the temerity to park my car in the club's official car park. Granted, taking the manager's space isn't the greatest way to start, but there we are! A telling off for playing the music too loud followed this and, to cap it all, blanking Phil Suarez when he came to offer some advice wasn't one of my best moves. In my defence, however, Phil had knocked the door of the tannoy box at the wrong time. Julian had told me that Phil would come to see me to give me a few pointers but, having only heard his dulcet tones from my usual position at the back of the Grange End in Ninian Park and never having met him, I was at a loss as to what Phil looked like. Furthermore, in the match build-up, a procession of people had knocked the door to forcibly offer their advice, i.e. don't play anything too loud or too modern and speak clearly and slowly at all times. A lot of them made it apparent that they also didn't much care for change, particularly when change meant accepting a ruffian from the Grange End, and one who had little in common with them other than a mutual love for all things Cardiff City.

When Phil eventually came to offer advice, I'd had enough of the numerous opinions thrust upon me. "Listen mate," I screamed at the poor fellow who'd walked into the small shed we called the tannoy box, "I've had enough of all this crap. Get out of my face, will you!" "Okay, no problem," he replied and sauntered off. A few seconds later, the penny dropped and I quickly went after him. "Um… excuse me," I spluttered, "but are you, by any chance, Phil Suarez?" "Yes," came the reply. "I'm really sorry. I can't believe I sent you packing. Can we start again, please?" Thankfully, Phil accepted my apology and came back to the tannoy box. He then went through everything with me, from how to work the equipment, what to say and when to say it, and how to deal with the culture shock of moving from the rough-and-ready Grange End to the more refined Grandstand.

Anyway, as with most pre-season friendlies, managers tended to try out most, if not all, of the fit players in their squad. This meant an array of substitutes, often double, triple or, as in the case of the Crystal Palace manager, Steve Bruce, six substitutes at a time. Not to be outdone, Alan Cork decided to go for multiple substitutions at a time as well. As you can imagine, this would have challenged the most capable stadium announcers. In my case, however, it was the beginning of a nightmare scenario.

Thankfully, I knew the Cardiff team well. On the other hand, scanning the Crystal Palace line-up for the day revealed another likely pitfall. How on earth was I going to pronounce names like: Aki Riihilahti, Fan Zhiyi, Jovan Kirovski or William Kwabena Antwi Agyei? Maybe I could wing it, I thought, who's to know! I'd forgotten one small thing. Among the 4,508 people in attendance were a sizeable number of Crystal Palace fans who knew their players' names and, more importantly, how to pronounce them.

As if to compound matters, a football-loving friend had volunteered to lend me a hand that day. However, the chap in question was an Arsenal fan from Stevenage and had no knowledge of either the Bluebirds or the Eagles. As you can imagine, it was a recipe for disaster.

My first blunder happened whilst trying to get my head around the four substitutes Cardiff's manager, Alan Cork, had decided to make at the same time. On they ran and off came four others. However, despite trying to keep up with the Fourth Official's board (a man who looked equally as flummoxed), I was lost after the second substitution and had completely forgotten the player that had left the field of play and his replacement. Furthermore, seeing another player making his way onto the pitch as two more left added to the confusion. I turned to my friend and asked, "Pete, who the hell were those last fellas, the ones before these ones? I ain't got a bloody clue anymore!" I could hear the laughter ring around the Grandstand. On looking up from the team sheet, I could see people pointing at me barely able to contain themselves. It was then that I realised that the microphone was still turned on.

Steve Bruce's substitutions for Crystal Palace caused even more mirth – this time among the away supporters. "Replacing Fan Zeezee," I boomed over the club's antiquated tannoy system, "is Akky Rakky Lakky!"

I couldn't wait for the game to end and, despite winning

the match 4–0 thanks to a Robert Earnshaw hat-trick and a goal from Graham Kavanagh, all I could think of was the many mistakes I had made. In fact, since that day I make it my business to check with the players or coaching staff, or the television and radio commentators that frequent matches, about pronunciations. In saying that, I'm not sure it helps that much as I still make mistakes.

Phil Suarez came over at the end of the game and reassured me that things were not as bad as I'd thought. Indeed, over the course of the next few months, Phil became a very good friend, always ready to reassure me that I was doing OK and always ready to offer advice if required. Sadly, he died a year later. Following his funeral, a Cardiff City fan used Phil's vivid and colourful commentaries to remix a song by a group called Collapsed Lung entitled 'Eat my goal'. It's a song I play from time to time as a tribute to him. Indeed, despite my often being referred to as the voice of Cardiff City, to me, the title will always belong to Phil Suarez, a real gent. RIP.

Many games have come and gone since that baptism of fire and I remember some of them for the oddest reasons. Take Blackpool in 2002. It comes to mind for a number of reasons. Firstly, the game was a bit of a sombre occasion as a friend's father had died in the week or two preceding the game and I had wanted to put a smile on my friend's face. Secondly, we'd had a new manager in Lennie Lawrence, after the club had sacked Alan Cork. And thirdly, I had just about had enough of the criticism aimed at me by some of the fans surrounding me in the Grandstand with regards to my style of announcing. In fairness, I went on to become good friends with many of them but a lot still didn't like 'the new bloke on the tannoy' or my choice of music. Suffice to say, I was determined to change their attitude towards me and the Blackpool game seemed as good a game as any to start with.

Around fifteen minutes before kick-off, I welcomed people to Ninian Park and announced that I had written a short prayer in honour of our owner, Sam Hammam. I then said that I would like to read it and asked people to be upstanding. To my complete surprise, people rose to their feet. "Crikey," I thought, "I'll have to do it now." I cleared my throat and somewhat nervously began:

> *Our Sam*
> *Who art at Ninian Park*
> *Hallowed be thy name*
> *As it was at Wimbledon*
> *Before thy sold it.*

I could hear a few giggles and continued:

> *Give us this season*
> *Our promotion,*

At this stage, fans started cheering:

> *And lead us not into relegation,*

Boos could be clearly heard around the ground. Indeed, it started to sound a bit like a pantomime. This was my cue to become more and more animated, taking on the mantra of an evangelical American preacher delivering a sermon:

And forgive us our coin throwing
As we forgive those that have thrown coins against us!

By now, Ninian Park was rocking with laughter:

And by the power of the Ayatollah!
And your cheque book
Forever and ever
Hammam.

Applause and laughter rang around the stadium in equal measure. Indeed, it egged me on to go further. "Ladies and gentlemen," I carried on, "I would like you all to turn to your hymn books now, also known as your matchday programme, and turn to page 442. However, if you have the old Alan Cork version, you may find this hymn on page 433… or page 424… or page 343… or page 334… or, if you have the original hymn book, on page 811." Of course, I was intimating towards the many changes we'd had in team formations and tactics, and the fans knew this immediately, laughing at every change in page or formation. I pressed play on the CD machine and out bellowed the music and lyrics of the hymn 'Kumbaya my Lord', which the City fans had changed to 'Sam Hammam, my Lord'.

As the song came to an end, I asked the fans to do the Ayatollah, Cardiff's legendary head tapping motion, and they obliged. However, the visiting Blackpool fans stood motionless, not quite sure how to respond to the unusual request emanating from the tannoy. This was my cue to pull their collective legs.

"Ladies and gentlemen," I began, "it seems we have been joined by some sinners! Yes, you people in orange! Come join us as I say, Blackpool, do the Ayatollah!" Blackpool fans stood stock-still as thousands of Cardiff fans booed them. "Brothers and sisters, no!" I shouted. "Forgive them, for they know not what they do! Show them what to do. Everyone, do the Ayatollah!" With this, Ninian Park again did the Ayatollah. "Now," I shouted again, "Blackpool, do the Ayatollah." This time, a solitary Blackpool fan joined in and applause and laughter rang out once again.

The response to my outburst was extraordinary. Most loved it. Indeed, such was the furore that Sam Hammam had created at the club that one of the fans even called for the prayer to be stuck onto the gates of Ninian Park. Being in the club's boardroom with the visiting chairman and associated directors of Blackpool, Sam hadn't actually heard the prayer dedicated to him and was a bit lost for words when people approached him about it. However, he called me a few days later with a mixture of surprise and astonishment that, as he put it, he'd found someone almost as crazy as himself. Indeed, it was the beginning of a great relationship and from then on Sam would occasionally call me or march into the tannoy box on a match day and encourage me to wind up the opposition's fans.

It has to be said that the club did receive a letter of complaint about Sam's prayer. This came from a vicar who had attended the Blackpool match. In fact, in his letter he complained that he had witnessed City lose by ten goals to nil yet had not been as offended as much as having to endure a desecration of the Lord's Prayer. In all honesty though, my aim was to entertain and certainly not to offend. With this in mind, I proposed apologising over the tannoy at the next game. However, after apologising to the Christians in attendance, I thought I'd better apologise to anyone of any other religion in attendance, just in case. I apologised to "all the Jews out there… to the Muslims… the Hindus… the Sikhs… to all you Buddhists… Rastafarians… the Bob Bank Hare Krishnas… the Grandstand Reconstructionists… I apologise to all the Canton Stand Yogi Jumpers… and the Grange End Tree Huggers. In fact, whatever your religion, may your God be with you!" To my astonishment, a round of applause could be heard from all four sides of Ninian Park.

It was hearing the laughter and applause in equal measure that decided my future approach to the tannoy at Ninian Park. From then on, I was determined to have as much fun with a microphone as was legally possible.

CHAPTER 4

It's fair to say that my father never understood my love of football. As an only child himself, I guess he was never much into team sports. In fact, during my own childhood, I remember receiving a lecture from him on the pointlessness of getting into the sport, telling me that football was nothing more than twenty-two grown men running aimlessly around a pitch for an hour and a half chasing a bag of wind!

I'm sure he thought my interest in football would be a passing fad and would probably wane after a few weeks. Nevertheless, my fascination with the beautiful game went from strength to strength. By the time my ninth birthday came around, Dad had given up all hope of dissuading me against the sport, but still tried to temper my enthusiasm. Other than West Ham and Aston Villa, most teams seemed to play in either blue or red and I was given the choice of a present of a shirt and shorts combination or a pair of football boots with socks. Whichever I preferred, the other would follow for my tenth birthday. I chose the boots and socks option and before long was the proud owner of a pair of Geoff Hurst football boots along with a pair of blue knee-length socks. From then on I spent hour upon hour wearing the plastic studs down on the concrete road surface a few streets from our Docks house, whacking balls against an array of local walls, to the great annoyance of the owners who, having allowed me a leeway of ten minutes to vent my frustrations on the side of their homes, often chased me away screaming expletives.

Thankfully, Dad never got wind of the neighbours' annoyance. Such was life back then that had anyone complained directly to him, I would probably have been grounded for life, my dreams of footballing stardom shattered into a myriad of pieces. Not that those dreams were anything other than the result of a vivid imagination. I mean, in my head I was a lion in defence who could run like a cheetah and leap like a gazelle. In reality, however, I had the defensive skills of a rabbit caught in headlights combined with the running skills of a tortoise and the leaping prowess of a hippo. On top of that, my physique as a youngster resembled that of an emaciated Barbie doll with an Afro. Nevertheless, I ate, drank and slept football. Sadly, I couldn't play it very well.

Needless to say, after a year of dreaming big, collecting cigarette cards, watching any football available on our black and white television screens, and spending hour upon hour smashing balls against irate neighbours' walls, Dad's patience with my new-found interest turned from mild irritation to total disdain. Suffice it to say, the shirt and shorts never materialised. I was gutted. That said, I couldn't blame him for not keeping his promise of a shirt and shorts. Even at a young age, I knew his priorities were a little more urgent than satisfying the whims of a football-mad youngster.

Dad had emigrated to Wales from Egypt in the late 1950s. He'd followed his father, a former merchant seaman, to the UK in order to study. I'm not sure he'd ever intended to stay. However, after returning to Egypt to marry in the early 1960s, he came back to complete his studies with my mother in tow. Children soon followed and before long there were eight of us, three adults and five kids, crammed into a three bedroom house in Margaret Street in Cardiff's Docklands. My parents occupied one bedroom, my grandfather another and, along with two brothers and two sisters, I shared the master bedroom of the house.

Back in the Sixties, the Docks were about as multicultural an area as was physically possible, a real melting pot. Later, I became aware that there had been almost fifty different nationalities living in the area at the time of my childhood, many having come to Wales via the sea and then settling close to it.

My closest group of friends had roots in Africa, Asia, North and Central America, the Caribbean and Europe, as well as sharing a working-class Cardiff identity. Each of us had our own unique language, culture and, more importantly, food. Indeed, as kids, all we cared for was football and our stomachs, often timing the ending of a local kick-about with lunch or dinner at the nearest friend's house, depending on what was on offer, be it curry, fried bananas or good old fish and chips. Also, there were very few cars in the area, so children often wandered the streets quite safely. Better still however, the dry docks, a stone's throw from our close-knit community, was the best playground any child could wish for.

Back then the dock was a working dock with ships arriving from all over the world. On top of that, every youngster in the area had at least one member of the family either working there or sailing on the ships being repaired. Health and safety was not so prevalent in those days and young boys and girls could wander over to watch the men at work. In fact, during my childhood, a number of local boys fell into the dry docks, their falls softened by the deep layers of mud that filled the dock. It didn't stop them going back though, even after having their stomachs pumped clean and receiving a customary clip around the ear.

Another thing I remember about the Docks is that doors were always left open and people often wandered in and out of each others homes. Also, every adult became a surrogate parent to the local kids, which in itself had its ups and downs. The advantages meant you could blag yourself an extra lunch or earn a few pennies tending a neighbour's garden or doing a few chores. On the downside, if you were cheeky to an adult, they had permission to punish you. That said, being punished by a neighbour was far more preferable to being punished by your own parents, which was guaranteed to hurt a lot more.

It's quite strange to wander around the area now – filled as it is with upmarket flats and tourists enjoying the many new restaurants and coffee shops that were once offices or Port Authority buildings. None of my peers ever expected the area to blossom in the way it has. It's certainly done wonders for the local economy. On reflection, however, there's a definite feel about the place that the soul of the area has been ripped away, replaced with a shiny, gleaming façade – a mish-mash of old meets new – aimed at showcasing Cardiff's aspirations as a modern, vibrant, dynamic capital city. Despite this, it's still where I feel I most belong. I'm just a Docks boy at heart.

Less than six months after beginning work at Ninian Park I was offered an opportunity to expand my horizons. As luck would have it, I was working in Swansea at the time when my mobile rang. "Son, if I was your club manager," began Julian Jenkins, "I'd say well done." "Why?" I asked. "You've been called up to serve your country," he replied.

To be completely honest, I was dumbfounded. Did they really know what they were taking on? Had they not heard some of the announcements I'd made? In fact, that was precisely the reason I'd been chosen. Apparently, a number of Football Association of Wales staff, season ticket holders at Ninian Park, thought I'd be perfect to help Mark Hughes take Wales into the World Cup finals.

With such lofty aspirations, my tenure with the Welsh FA began with a friendly against Argentina at the Millennium Stadium. Unlike Cardiff City matches, I was required to attend pre-match meetings with Millennium Stadium officials to go over crowd safety issues and their implications on the stadium's public address system. The meetings were chaired by Paul Sergeant, now the Chief Executive at Llanelli Scarlets Rugby Club, who managed Wales' premier stadium, and his able assistant was none other than the former Welsh rugby international and Llanelli legend, Rupert Moon.

Over the six years I spent announcing at Welsh internationals at the stadium, I grew to love working with Paul and Rupert. Paul was a warm, no-nonsense type of manager while Rupert's stage management of events was second to none. However, my first dealing with him was awkward to say the least.

I'd arrived at the Millennium Stadium with plenty of time to set up, having put together at least two hours' worth of music to cover pre-match, half-time and the end of the game. I'd also prepared a script of sorts, with various trivia facts about football in Argentina and an array of stats on the players of both teams: their appearance records, goals scored, regional clubs, etc.

Anyway, after meeting the PA technicians, a mobile phone was handed to me by a lady called Anne, one of the stadium's management team. On the other end of the line was Rupert Moon. "Now look here!" he began, "we've heard all about you! Let's get something straight, this is not Ninian Park!" I was a bit taken aback and, if I'm completely honest, a bit miffed. There I was, about to make my international tannoy debut for Wales, being berated by a legend from the world of Welsh rugby. What happened next still makes me smile. Maybe it was the Docks boy in me or the hurt pride kicking in or possibly both but I handed the phone back to Anne and simply remarked, "I think he's got the wrong number." Anne looked at me in complete shock and put the phone to her ear. "Rupert," she said, "he's given me the phone back." On finishing her conversation she put the phone in her pocket, looked pensively at me and said that Rupert was on his way to see me, before making a quick exit.

At this point, especially after seeing Anne disappear back up the tunnel, I paused to question whether it was such a good idea to blank a man that had represented Wales at rugby. I mean, call it bravado, but it's easy to be brave when you're speaking on a phone. It's something altogether different, foolish even, being disrespectful to a former international scrum-half when he's stood facing you. Indeed, it was at that very moment that the thought of a giant of a man who enjoyed taking a hit or two and who enjoyed doing the hitting himself suddenly came to mind. I quickly dismissed such negative thoughts and looked around for any heavy objects that might come in handy. There were none except the microphone I was holding. That said, I could hardly use a microphone as a weapon. I mean, imagine getting arrested for attempting to assault a former Welsh rugby international with a microphone. Anyway, what possible damage could be done with a microphone! I suppose I could try announcing him into submission.

As Rupert approached, I composed myself. He had looked quite big from a distance. With each stride towards me, I realised that I had totally underestimated his size. He was far bigger than I'd expected. In fact, he was massive.

Thinking on my feet, I took a deep intake of breath and tried to make myself look equally as big, if not fearless at least. As he stomped his way towards me, I forced myself to stop shaking and extended a hand. "Er... hello Rupert! It's... um... good to meet you... yeah, er... tidy!" I stammered. Composing myself, I continued. "Was that really you on the phone? I thought it was someone winding me up," I said trying desperately to look innocent. His scowl turned to a smile. "Welcome to the Millennium Stadium," he said, shaking my hand with a vice-like grip and knowing full well that I was being a bit conservative with the truth.

Rupert was a true gentleman from that point on and a real professional. He went through my playlist and schedule and helped plan the event so that it would run as smoothly as possible, offering advice but never trying to take over.

That first international was quite surreal. I couldn't quite believe my luck. Not only did I have access to the Millennium Stadium's inner sanctum – I was also within touching distance of the likes of Ryan Giggs, Craig Bellamy, John Hartson, Juan Sebastián Verón, Caniggia, Riquelme, Julio Ricardo Cruz and Kily González. These were players I'd only ever seen on television or from the upper reaches (or cheap seats) in the Arms Park. At the time, the Argentina team were the World Cup favourites. There were perks to this announcing malarkey after all.

As the crowd filtered into the stadium, my first job that evening was to introduce the RAF St Athan Voluntary Band, a brass band with a long history of playing at major rugby events. I'd agreed with their director of music, Alan, that although the band would perform the national anthems, it was pointless to march around the pitch playing, as very few inside would hear them, such were the acoustics of the Millennium Stadium. As a makeshift, I would play the stirring anthem of 'Men of Harlech' over the tannoy, as a way of an entrance for them. I don't think anyone had ever asked them to march onto the pitch in complete silence before and he muttered something along the lines of, "we always get to perform live at the rugby".

Despite our tenuous agreement, Alan had had a change of mind and, as the band marched onto the pitch, out boomed 'Men of Harlech'. It was bizarre. 'Men of Harlech' could be heard over the tannoy and here was another version, in a completely different key, on the pitch. I suppose you could call it 'in for a penny, in for a pound' because once in place, such was the band's insistence on performing live, that they then began playing a repertoire of the songs they'd usually play at rugby games. By now, the music I was playing over the stadium's public address system had moved on to songs from the Stereophonics and Catatonia, while the RAF band played traditional Welsh songs such as 'Calon Lân' and 'We'll Keep a Welcome in the Hillside'. It must have sounded like a schizophrenic club DJ had been double-booked to play a gig for an 18 to 30 holiday and a day centre for pensioners, and had decided to try to cater for both at the same time.

I was at a complete loss at to what to do and, shy of turning the tannoy off, there wasn't much I could do. It was at this moment that Paul Sergeant stepped in. With a few telling hand gestures to its musical director, the band stopped playing.

It's fair to say that that night set a pattern I've followed ever since – that is, with regard to the occasional occupational hazard of every PA announcer: mistakes, better described as gaffes. I guess mistakes happen in all walks of life. You just have to deal with them. In terms of the tannoy, it's getting a scorer wrong, mispronouncing names or finding yourself going off on a tangent and unable to dig a way out other than to simply stop talking.

Most announcers, of course, try their hardest to sound slick and professional. Indeed, many come from local radio backgrounds. However, as hard as I try, there has always been an element to my personality that often causes me to make mistakes in the full glare of others. In fact, when I think about it, from childhood to adulthood, I've always seemed to make my biggest gaffes in front of others and have been the subject of much ribbing accordingly. Matters aren't helped either by a lifelong general slowness to catch on.

That evening, excitement certainly got the better of me. Maybe it was the fact that due to a Craig Bellamy goal, Wales were leading the World Cup favourites. Anyway, having successfully negotiated a birthday list which included some of the most Welsh-sounding names known to mankind, from Goronwy Jones and Angharad Gruffudd to Mererid ap Williams and Celyn Haf Phillips, confidence got the better of me and I began ad-libbing, adding that I hoped all those celebrating their birthday that day were enjoying our win against Argentina. Laughter began to filter back from the stands.

As opposed to my shed at Ninian Park, the tannoy position in the Millennium Stadium is behind the home bench, therefore, in the middle of the fans. Worse still, the fans that tend to sit behind the PA announcer are usually kids blowing furiously on plastic horns. It took a while to fathom why the horns had gone quiet and why people were laughing so much around me. "What's the big joke?" I thought.

Finally, the penny dropped – it was only half-time!

There was no hiding place and the more I tried explaining my gaffe away, the more I dug a bigger hole for myself, encountering more laughter in the process. I gave up and sat back down. With this, a group of young teens in Cardiff City shirts sitting directly behind the tannoy, plastic horns in hand, began prodding me. As I turned to face them, they looked me straight in the eye and began chanting, "You're shit and you know you are!"

CHAPTER 6

At Ninian Park, it seemed that the more I pushed boundaries on the tannoy, the more I created a rod for my own back – as more was never quite enough for some of our fans, or our owner – much to the horror of those whose remit was keep order. And despite the numerous telling-offs from the police and stewards, the positive feedback I was getting from those that mattered to me, i.e. Sam Hammam and the Bluebirds supporters, focussed my mind on changing the way tannoys were used at football forever. Never again, in my mind, was the PA system just for reading team sheets and playing a bit of incidental music. In fact, I began thinking of it as a way not only to express myself but also to reflect the feelings of the entire Cardiff City fan base, particularly towards visiting teams or anything that appeared in the local and national press involving the club. We were building a bit of a siege mentality and I was on a mission to express it vocally. I scoured newspapers and messageboards for ideas, spent hours on Google looking for funny announcements to adapt and downloaded song after song whose lyrics had a line or two that reflected a particular storyline or opinions among the fans or, indeed, had a tenuous link to a visiting team. Nothing was out of bounds and everything was considered fair game.

It must have been quite frustrating for the safety staff at the time, as few of them had any inkling as to what they were going to hear from week to week. That said, few were also aware of the amount of preparation that went into trying to create a bit of banter. In fact, to this day, a lot of people still think I just turn up and make it up as I go along. If only! Mind you, I dare say it might sound like that sometimes.

Part of the process of changing the way things were done on the PA was by conducting some research on how others took to their task as tannoy announcers. And for that reason, I became friendly with a number of other announcers around the country, shadowing quite a few to get some tips. One of those was Paul Burrell at Arsenal. In one respect, Paul could easily be described as PA royalty. He was a regular at Wembley, particularly for England internationals, and had worked on Champions League and UEFA Cup matches, FA Cup semis and finals and League Cup finals.

Paul had invited me to watch him in action at Highbury for an Arsenal versus Chelsea match. However, it came as quite a surprise when I got there to see him glued to a television screen cheering on Birmingham as they took on local rivals Aston Villa. He was born and raised in the Midlands and, despite working for Arsenal for over fifteen years, confessed to being a Birmingham fan at heart, even more so a Chasetown fan, often working for the non-league club when Arsenal were away from home.

Prior to kick-off, Paul gave me an impromptu tour of Highbury and introduced me to a number of ex-players and staff, culminating in an introduction to Arsenal's manager, Arsene Wenger. In fact, Arsene Wenger ushered me into his office to watch Paul conduct an interview with him for inclusion in their pre-match build up on the giant screens in the stadium. I've met Arsene Wenger twice since then and, to date, consider him the nicest manager in football.

Nevertheless, it was quite clear that Paul was held in high esteem at Arsenal and was the consummate professional. Indeed, I learned a lot just by watching him at work. In one way though, Paul's style epitomised everything I wasn't. I guess working in the Premiership, especially at a top club like Arsenal, meant sticking to a rigid set-up of official announcements and sponsor messages with very few opportunities to create a bit of banter. It was a shame really because he had a great sense of humour.

Funnily enough, it was also at Highbury that I made my impromptu debut on Sky TV, not that Sky TV had any say in the matter.

I had received an all-areas pass from Paul, meaning that apart from the changing rooms I had access to almost anywhere in Highbury. Therefore I decided to go down to the pitch-side near one of the corner flags to savour the atmosphere. As it happened I was spotted by a mate watching television back in Cardiff. He phoned to say that he could see me and dared me to do something to get noticed. With my phone still in hand, the chance came a few moments later as Thierry Henry took a corner right in front of me. As he prepared to launch the ball towards the Chelsea box, over his shoulder I was jumping about frantically, tapping my head doing the famous Cardiff City Ayatollah, not quite sure what Henry would make of it if he had turned around. All the same, I could hear my mate laughing down the line and shouting instructions, "left a bit, left a bit… no, too far… right a bit now, down a bit. Yes, stay there!" Several of the Arsenal stewards looked on in bemusement. One, however, approached me. "You're a Cardiff fan, aren't you!" he exclaimed. "Yes," I replied, "how did you know?" "I'm from Barry," he said laughing, "It was the Ayatollah that gave you away."

Having thoroughly enjoyed my day at Arsenal I jumped at the chance to visit other grounds. Another opportunity came along a few weeks later while working for HTV Wales in Leeds.

The set-up at Leeds was quite different to Arsenal in that they had three people working on their tannoy – one to play music, another to control the scoreboard and an Irish lad called Dara doing the announcements.

At the time Leeds were sitting pretty on top of the Premier Division and were regularly attracting 40,000 plus to their home games. That day, Leeds were taking on Chelsea and Elland Road was completely sold out. Like Paul at Arsenal, Dara gave me a tour of the stadium and introduced me to the rest of the tannoy lads, and, as luck would have it, to their Chief Executive, Peter Ridsdale. Incidentally, a highlight for me that day was also meeting one of their most famous former players, the late, great John Charles, who still lived in the area and often attended their games.

Dara made most of his announcements with a radio microphone on the pitch so, while he did this, I sat in one of the dugouts taking in the atmosphere and waited for him to finish. Unfortunately, however, after he'd introduced the teams onto the pitch he'd forgotten I was still there, that was, until Claudio Ranieri tried to take his seat and saw me sitting in it. Dara quickly ran over and apologised to the Chelsea manager who joked in broken English that he thought for a minute that he'd lost his job.

Space was at a premium in the tannoy box, so I watched

the game from one of the stands, which was no bad thing as it meant getting close to the Leeds supporters, particularly their more vociferous element. If truth be told, Leeds fans seemed much like Cardiff fans. They were very passionate about their club and very vocal with it. In saying that, one of the things that struck me about them was the amount of pies the Leeds fans consumed. In fact, if they weren't chanting, they were eating. I thought Cardiff fans liked their pies but Elland Road took the eating of pies to a whole new level. It was, without doubt, the pie-scoffing capital of the football world. Almost every one of them had a pie in their hand, so much so, that I felt quite naked without one.

As luck would have it, a few months after that game we drew Leeds in the FA Cup, which gave me a chance to invite Dara to Ninian Park. It was also an opportunity to try some new things on the tannoy, particularly knowing it would be a full house. Nevertheless, as a precautionary measure, I phoned Dara to check whether or not Leeds fans would object to a bit of banter. He reassured me that they would appreciate any kind of laugh. If he'd have known what I had in mind I think his answer would have been a firm 'no'!

With the help of a DJ friend, I downloaded their club song, 'Marching on Together', and set to work remixing it with a few choice sentences from the Monty Python 'Four Yorkshiremen' sketch. For good measure, we also remixed Hot Chocolate's 'You Sexy Thing' with sheep sounds and transferred a number of sound effects, television themes and jingles to a CD for possible inclusion. I couldn't wait to see the reaction.

Knowing the interest in the game I'd left the car at home that cold January afternoon and decided to walk the couple of miles to the ground. The local pubs on my route were packed out, buzzing with excitement. It was our biggest game in many a year and it seemed that everyone in Cardiff wanted a piece of the action.

Inside the ground, as the Leeds players took to the pitch to warm up, many had already made their way onto the Ninian Park terraces, intent on giving them an intimidating welcome. The boos and jeers whistling around the ground were my cue to hit play on our first remix – 'Marching on Together' Cardiff-style and, as the song rang around Ninian Park, Cardiff fans began staring at the tannoy box in disbelief, not quite able to fathom why on earth I was playing Leeds Utd's anthem. In fact, neither could the Leeds fans. Delighted at hearing their favourite song, they began singing it in unison. However, after one verse and one comedy scratch sound later, the anthem took an altogether different twist and out boomed the voice of John Cleese, "who'd have thought thirty year ago we'd all be sittin' here drinking Château de Chasselas, eh?" The Leeds fans, and their players, stood in complete bewilderment. Thousands of Cardiff fans, on the other hand, laughed.

Another song that took on a whole new meaning that day was Dario G's 'Hey Baby'. It had been played for most of the season but adapted by Cardiff fans, as the day got nearer, to suit the fact that one of Leeds' players, Lee Bowyer, had escaped a prison sentence for an alleged assault on an Asian lad. As soon as the song hit the airwaves, to a man, Cardiff fans began chanting, "Hey Lee Bowyer… we wanna know why you're not in jail!"

Next came the team sheets and once I'd gone through the home team, it was time to read the visitors starting line-up. As I pressed play on Antonin Dvořák's *New World Symphony*, also known as the Hovis advert music, it was obvious by then that the Leeds players were getting rattled by the reception they were getting from the home fans. "Number one," I bawled, "aye oop... that'll be Nigel Martyn... number two... aye oop... that'll be Gary Kelly." I continued through the Leeds line-up. The jeers grew louder and louder. There was no let up. Leeds knew they'd be in a match.

It was to be an unforgettable day in the football club's history, especially when the team came back from a goal behind to record a 2–1 win and knock the Premier Division leaders out of the FA Cup. On the negative side, a mini pitch invasion celebrating the win threatened to turn to violence as a section of the Cardiff support headed for their Leeds counterparts. Thankfully, the police were on hand to quell any disturbance.

After the game, journalists used the threat of violence as an excuse to blame Sam Hammam for the intimating atmosphere, claiming that he had added fuel to the fire by winding the Leeds fans up using the club's tannoy. In fairness to him though, I hadn't given Sam any inkling of what I was going to do. Indeed, I made sure that Sam knew nothing in case my feathers were clipped. However, such was the vitriol from the press, I thought I might lose my job over it. A few days later, Sam phoned. "Ali, baby! You are as crazy as me. Keep it up!"

CHAPTER 7

Every football-mad schoolboy dreams of playing for their favourite team and every football-loving adult dreams of working for theirs. However, to some fans, staff at football clubs can be a bit like Marmite – they either love them or hate them. And some of the staff at football clubs sometimes feel the same way towards some supporters as well.

In all honesty though, the buzz of working for your favourite club can soon wear off. Most of all, it's an emotional rollercoaster. The mood around the club is almost always determined by the results on the field. If the team wins, you can guarantee a lot of smiling faces around the place, but if they lose, a trip to the office can be like entering a morgue.

I guess I've learned to take the good with the bad when it comes to Cardiff City. I mean, let's face it, most of my life it's been mediocre. That said, I've become used to the highs and lows. I've also become good friends with many of Cardiff City's staff. It's safe to say though that that wasn't always the case, especially when I first started, partly due to being the new kid on the block and in part due to having what is politely described as a strong character. Others just call it pig-headedness.

If, however, I had to single out any group of colleagues that have caused the greatest amount of angst and joy in equal measure, then it has to be the club's stewards and security staff. Whether it's being on the receiving end of a lecture on where I could or couldn't park my car or being constantly told to turn the tannoy volume up or down depending on who was complaining or, indeed, having my access to various parts of the ground restricted – never has so much grief been given by so many to so few, i.e. me. In saying that, many of them are now good mates. Some I consider to be the absolute salt of the earth, one or two will never be on my Christmas card list but we've learned to live with each other. For the first few years though, the relationship was tense, to say the least, made all the more unpalatable by an incident that some will never forget – 'Stokegate'

'Stokegate' was a kiss of death announcement made by a member of the stewarding staff (I won't embarrass him by putting his name here) ten minutes before the end of a crucial League One play-off semi-final against Stoke City, a match in which the Bluebirds were winning on aggregate at the time. After declining to make the announcement myself, the steward in question took to the airwaves to inform Cardiff fans that the team would come back out to do a 'lap of honour'. The point of the announcement was to try to keep the pitch in pristine condition for a forthcoming FAW Cup final match against Swansea and, to counter a possible, although customary, pitch invasion should the team register a win. After all, we were winning at the time. As things stood, however, the words would come back to haunt not only the perpetrator, but me as well. Within a couple of minutes of the announcement, Stoke had equalised. Extra-time followed and the inevitable happened, Stoke won the game, leaving the club, and me, with egg on our face.

The backlash was incredible. No matter how many times I declared my innocence, nobody seemed to believe me.

Nasty emails, texts and phone calls kept coming. Just as galling, the person responsible kept his head down, happy for me to take the blame. I guess the hurt and numbness after that match affected everyone, me included, and people were analysing the match in every possible detail, looking for any reason to explain our capitulation. Worse still for me, the club's captain, Graham Kavanagh, a former Stoke player, made a point about the announcement in the local press, saying that it acted as a catalyst to the opposition and nullified the home team. Cue more abuse. With all due respect to Kav, I thought blaming the loss on an announcement was a bit of a lame excuse – an easy way out for the players.

And so, following that debacle, and to a lesser extent previous experiences, I was on a mission to embarrass the stewards over the tannoy as often as I could.

The first opportunity came at the FAW Cup final match. Again, following orders from the League regarding pitch invasions, I was asked to put a polite message out to request that fans kept off the playing surface. I waited until the ground had filled.

"Ladies and gentlemen," I began, "at the end of tonight's match we request that you stay off the pitch. Indeed, we have assembled a team of crack ninja-trained stewards who will eject anyone who attempts to get on the pitch. Let me warn you that these stewards do not know the meaning of the word 'fear'. In fact, like all our stewards, they don't know the meaning of most words."

On and on it went with each game providing another chance to have a pop at the stewards. "Ladies and gentlemen, here at Cardiff City Football Club we have some of the best stewards in the country. Unfortunately, none of them are working today."

"There may be fifty ways to leave your lover, but there are only four ways to leave Ninian Park. On exiting, please be sure to take all your belongings. Anything left behind will probably be distributed amongst the stewards. Therefore, please do not leave children or spouses."

"Thank you for attending today's match, and remember, nobody loves you, or your lost possessions, more than Cardiff City's stewards."

"We've received a number of complaints about our stewards. In fact, some of you are saying that they are perfect idiots, however, let me reassure you that they are not perfect yet, but they are doing their very best."

"Apologies to our visiting fans. Your delay in exiting Ninian Park this evening is caused by the some of our stewards suffering from elbow and backside syndrome, not knowing their elbows from their backsides. I'll let you have any further information as soon as I'm given any."

"Ladies and gentlemen, please respect our stewards. Ordinary people live and learn. They just live."

For some reason, a few of the stewards and security staff are still a bit cagey towards me. Beats me why!

Over the years, a lot of the security and stewarding staff have become good friends of mine. Indeed, on match days, I look forward to seeing them as much as I look forward to the football itself. I guess, all things aside, we all love the club in our own way and, although all our jobs have their ups and downs, working at the stadium is more of a pleasure than it will ever be a chore.

Talking of staff, I can't let this chapter go without giving a few others a mention. Some are still at the club, others are not but it's safe to say that all have had an influence over the tannoy in one way or another.

I'll start with the two who've kept me on the straight and narrow at Cardiff City, Julian Jenkins, who was responsible for giving me the job in the first place, and Wayne Nash.

Julian has held several positions in the club, from a fans' liaison officer and the club's media manager to head of ticketing and customer relations. Wayne, on the other hand, the longest-serving member of staff at the club, worked his way up from being a member of the ground staff to become the club's stadium manager. Both have had their fair share of flak over the years, especially from irate fans looking for scapegoats but both, without a doubt, are the kind of people without whom Cardiff City simply couldn't function. Also, despite stretching their patience over the years, both have supported me through thick and thin. Time after time, both have also gone way beyond their job descriptions to help others: from conducting ad hoc guided tours of the stadium for Cardiff City-mad children, to introducing star-struck supporters to their idols, organising signed shirts and balls for charity raffles, and providing tickets for individuals or groups that have travelled from afar to watch their beloved Bluebirds. Nothing has ever been too much trouble for them. Indeed, the club has won a number of prestigious industry awards, in no small part due to the work they and their teams do.

Another colleague I hold in high regard is Wayne Crichton – also known as Half-time Wayne or Insane Wayne, one of the world's genuine nice guys. Fans are sometimes described as Cardiff City-mad and Wayne definitely falls in that category. He lives, breathes and sleeps Cardiff City and will do anything for the club, whether doing his stint as a half-time announcer, club photographer or helping out with the media department. In fact, if you asked him to drive the team bus I dare say he'd give it a go. He's also forever dipping into his own pocket; indeed, such is his generosity that Wayne even paid for the music equipment in the new stadium's PA room. On top of that, for all the work he does, he's never received or asked for a penny in return. I guess, in terms of the tannoy, he's about as unlikely a partner as I could get, and we're often compared to an old married couple. I wouldn't swap him for anyone else.

There are plenty more I enjoy seeing, whether on a match day or not, including the club's ticket office staff, ground staff, receptionists, office staff, club shop staff and laundry ladies. In fact, when I think about it, the club is full of colourful characters, from top to bottom.

One of Ninian Park's endearing qualities was its ability to bring all the staff together: players, management, full- and part-time staff alike. This was mainly due to the fact that the club's canteen facilities were open to all (and the food was subsidised). You could eat, share a joke and catch up on the latest gossip. No cliques ever existed either. Indeed, you could find yourself chatting to the manager, a player, a coach, a member of the sales team, the stadium manager and an accountant all on the same table. Alas, the new stadium has no such facility, which means that staff in different departments rarely mix on a daily basis. I guess change is never always a good thing. That said, one individual who had really looked forward to moving to the new stadium but sadly died a short while before, was a man that was highly respected among the staff and fans alike. His name was Jeff Richards.

Jeff was a former police officer who began his career when policemen were a physical presence on the terraces. He was probably best described as 'old school', a no-nonsense big-hearted man who gave people the benefit of the doubt but had little time for idiots. I'd seen and known of Jeff since I was a teenager, often bumping into him on Ninian Park's Bob Bank or Grange End terraces, as well as the odd sighting at away games. In fact, I'd spent most of my youth trying to avoid him and his colleagues as I tried to get into Ninian Park without paying. However, it was after starting work on the tannoy much later in life that I really got to know him, and was very glad I did too.

Jeff's dry sense of humour was infectious and, from time to time, he'd ask me to pass on his best wishes to a variety of people over the tannoy, especially those he'd had the pleasure of arresting during his time as a police officer. One of those was Frank Humphries, a tough ex-hooligan and former adversary of his, but a Bluebird through and through nonetheless. I would have loved to have seen Frank's face when he heard Jeff wishing him a happy 60th birthday. Then again, knowing Frank as I do, I think he would have appreciated it all the same.

Reading an eulogy for Jeff was probably one of the

hardest things I've ever had to do on the tannoy. Jeff would probably have told me to pull myself together and to stop being such a wimp, but you could almost hear a pin drop as I read the tribute to him, such was the respect held for him. It was also lovely to see the pitch at Ninian Park surrounded by stewards, with his family in attendance to witness the affection for him. At the end of the tribute, his name was chanted by all four sides of the ground, "There's only one Jeff Richards!"

Jeff had talked about the move in terms of a new era for the club. In a way though, it was fitting that he'd always be associated with Ninian Park. As way of a lasting tribute to Jeff, the club named its Control Room after him, adorning the wall outside with his picture. Also, we hold an annual charity match – Police v Stewards – in his memory.

RIP Jeff, much missed and much loved.

CHAPTER 8

Following the FA Cup win over Leeds, music became a great way of getting subtle, and sometimes blatantly obvious, messages across. In fact, the playlist was fast becoming a musical newspaper, often reflecting my own and other fans' weekly thoughts of goings-on in and around Cardiff City Football Club.

As daft as it sounds, I've never been one for remembering results, but I have remembered games for some of the strangest reasons, like a ball whacking someone in the face or someone streaking across the pitch. I now also remember games for the laughs I've had on the tannoy and, it seems, so do others.

A game that I'm constantly reminded of was a Championship match against West Ham.

I suppose I'd always had a bit of a love/hate relationship with West Ham. On the one hand I loved them for having one of the UK's first black players, Clyde Best, a childhood hero of mine, and for the fact that my first ever football boots were a pair of Geoff Hurst boots – possibly one of the first brand endorsements. On the other hand, I hated West Ham, on account of a local lad who supported them, and his constant belittling of Cardiff City. This, despite the fact that the lad in question was Cardiff born and bred, and the fact that his hatred of his local side seemed to have no end, no matter how well the Bluebirds did. And boy did he like everyone knowing his opinion! If we were promoted, we were lucky and if we were relegated, we deserved it.

Indeed, such was his devotion to the Hammers that he no longer used his own name and instead got people to call him West Ham. In fact, I wouldn't have been surprised if he had changed his name to West Ham by deed poll. On top of that, he lived near me in Grangetown, one of the heartlands of Cardiff City support in the capital. However, his house was painted claret and blue in honour of his favourite team, and he'd adorned his front door with glass that contained West Ham's club badge. I guess I should admire him for his commitment but, after visiting Upton Park and witnessing the sheer hatred some West Ham fans had for Cardiff City and, for that matter, all things Welsh – West Ham would forever become one of those clubs I loved to hate.

Anyway, I wasn't sure he'd go to the game, an evening kick-off, but I knew for certain that he'd sit with the away supporters if he did. This was my chance for a bit of payback.

I guess my choice of music was also dictated by the fact that we had had a bit of history with West Ham with regard to violence at matches. Indeed, as a youngster, I remember quite clearly the fighting that used to take place at Ninian Park every time the Hammers were in town. Times had changed, however, and I merely wanted to create a bit of banter between the opposing fans. Most bought into it. In fact, apart from 'You can't touch this' by MC Hammer, featuring the line "stop! Hammer time", most of the songs were quite lame, possibly containing the odd reference to the evening's game. One example was Nat King Cole's 'Let's face the music' with an opening line of "there may be trouble ahead". Another was the Clash's 'I fought the law'. Also included was the theme from the BBC comedy *Steptoe and Son* (and yes, I know they're from Shepherd's Bush i.e. QPR territory) along with an announcement for the owner of a shire horse answering to name of Hercules, which was attached to a rag-and-bone cart and left unattended in the club car park, to please return to their vehicle.

Added to the playlist was crooner Max Bygraves, Ian Dury with 'Hit me with your rhythm stick' and Smiley Culture's 'Cockney Translation' as well as one of my pre-match favourites – a song called 'Cockney Medley' by Bill Bailey; a collection of pop songs, including Survivor's 'Eye of the Tiger', Prodigy's 'Firestarter' (or Cockney Firestarter, as Bill Bailey put it), Cliff Richard's 'Devil Woman' and Chris Rea's 'Lady in Red', all mixed together in the style of a Cockney knees-up.

It was meant to be a laugh, however, the consequences of my actions resulted in a campaign by a *Sun* journalist to try to get me sacked, claiming that I was intent on creating trouble between both sets of fans. Me? Never! Thankfully, however, most of the away fans saw the funny side including West Ham's own directors, who subsequently invited me to Upton Park for the return fixture. On top of that, Sam Hammam stuck by me. I still laugh at the idea that Nat King Cole or *Steptoe and Son* could be blamed for antisocial behaviour. Nevertheless, it turned out to be a great night for Cardiff City, winning the game 4–1. Talk about hammer time! (Forgive the pun.)

After the West Ham game, my email inbox was overloaded with suggestions for other teams. For Stoke, it had to be Elvis Presley's 'The wonder of you', which just happens to be Port Vale's anthem, their arch rivals. When the Black Cats of Sunderland visited, Tom Jones' 'What's new pussycat?' blared out at them, along with a number of songs associated with their rivals, Newcastle. Blackpool were welcomed with George Formby's 'With my little stick of Blackpool rock' and Brighton had everything from 'It's raining men' and 'I want to take you to a gay bar' to 'YMCA' and 'Dancing Queen'. In fact, almost every team who visited Ninian Park that season were greeted with a range of songs aimed at poking harmless fun at them. On the whole, I'd say that visiting fans enjoyed the experience. It certainly made a change from the drab chart music too often cloned and blasted out at other grounds, and meant a trip to Cardiff was something altogether different.

CHAPTER 9

As much as I love working on the tannoy, I do miss standing among my old terrace friends, whether it's singing along with them to favourite songs and chants, nattering away about the beautiful game or just watching in nervous expectation of better things to come. I guess it's made all the more special by knowing that the person next to you is probably going through exactly the same emotions.

With four demanding children, three of whom are girls, I also miss travelling to away games on a regular basis. Part of the early attraction of football for me was that there was always something special about travelling to away games with Cardiff City. I suppose you made more of an effort to enjoy yourself at away games. Also, we're not exactly the most sedate of fans, often taking over entire motorway service stations no matter who else was using the facilities, be they other football fans or unsuspecting families desperate for a toilet stop. And, on certain trips, we tended to travel in large numbers, especially to games in London.

I've never really understood the attraction of London compared to other destinations, particularly when most of the time is spent in traffic to and from the games. Also, Cup and now Championship games apart, London-based teams in the lower leagues: Orient, Brentford etc., held little appeal. Nevertheless, Cardiff fans still travelled there in large numbers.

Looking back, one London game I'll never forget, for all the wrong reasons, was a Division Two trip to Fulham which took place at the beginning of the 1993/94 season. The club had won the new Division Three championship the previous season and, coupled with the excitement of a new season and fresh start, over 3,000 fans headed for Fulham's Craven Cottage ground.

In my case, the journey was all the more eventful having spent the best part of it, along with five others, squashed into the back of a small delivery van driven by a friend of a friend, Darren – a man who's driving style could at best be described as kamikaze, at worst, completely reckless. In fact, it was probably a good thing that the van had no rear or side windows. Feeling the van swerve from side to side as Darren leant out to shout abuse at fans of other clubs that had had the temerity to overtake him, was enough in itself. Suffice to say, arriving in London in one piece was a relief in itself. The game was merely a bonus.

I guess one of my most endearing memories of that journey to Craven Cottage was meeting Eddie the punk. Eddie was a Chelsea fan who was a mate of one of the lads in the van and had wanted to tag along, especially if it meant getting involved in an altercation with Fulham fans. I suppose I should have guessed by Darren's earlier behaviour on the motorway that the group I had travelled with, which included a lad and his girlfriend, were not your average football fans, that is, apart from myself and the friend that had persuaded me to go in the van. Also, I couldn't quite work out why Eddie wanted to join us for a game against Fulham. Everybody knew that Fulham revelled in the tag of being a family club and Craven Cottage was definitely a ground that was more used to dealing with the more happy-clappy type of supporter.

Anyway, after meeting Eddie near a local pub, we headed into the ground. As kick-off approached, it became apparent that Fulham's stewards were having major problems accommodating the large number of away fans that had descended on them from south Wales. So much so they decided to offer entry to their family stand to any Cardiff fan who didn't wish to wait. I remember looking over and thinking there were an awful lot of Cardiff fans in with the Fulham fans, but relations between both sets of fans seemed to be well humoured.

In the official away end, the Putney End, Eddie the punk was in his element. He'd already learned how to do the Ayatollah and loved the banter batted to and fro between the Cardiff fans in both stands. Within a few minutes of the game starting, however, everything changed.

Normally, I tend to ignore fighting at games and try to watch the match. After all, what was the point of travelling all that way just to watch a punch-up? I could do that on a Saturday night in Cardiff. I certainly needn't go to London for it. This was different though, as three of our party – Darren in particular – along with Eddie the punk, a lad called Mike and a few hundred others, jumped the fence and raced over to Fulham's family stand. I guess some of Fulham's hooligans (yes, they have them too) had taken umbrage with Cardiff fans being in one of their stands and had made their way from another part of the ground to ambush a few. And, as the two sets of fans got stuck into each other, the game came to a halt, leaving me and my friend watching our driver take a pelting and wondering if we needed to find a lift home.

Thankfully, Darren escaped arrest and only one of our party was frogmarched away by the police (two including Eddie the punk who, because of his London accent, was mistaken for a home fan and thrown in a cell with the Fulham hooligans). That said, we still had to hang about outside the local police station until 8 p.m. for the release of the Cardiff lad, Mike, whose bravado saw him discharged with a badly bruised face minus his NHS glasses. As for Eddie, I never saw him again. Suffice to say, I have never travelled in Darren's van since. I don't think my nerves could take it

The Fulham game had ended in a 3–1 win for the City, with the Bluebirds scoring all the goals in the match thanks to an own-goal by Lee Baddeley. However, the trip reminded me of the precarious nature of away games during the 1980s and, at certain times, the likelihood of violence if you found yourself in the wrong place at the wrong time – especially for a skinny, bespectacled black teenager from Cardiff.

There were times when being a skinny, bespectacled black teenager had its advantages, particularly on trips to other multicultural cities in the UK such as Bristol, Birmingham or Nottingham. Moreover, it meant that I could meander around cities without too much trouble, although this wasn't always the case.

On one trip, an FA Cup match at Leicester's old Filbert Street ground on New Year's Day in 1981, a game that ended in a depressing 3–0 loss for the team, I can remember mixing quite freely with the home fans for a good hour before kick-off and sauntering into the away end in a carefree mood. The mood soon changed. As I walked in, I was greeted with the chant, "There's only one wog in Cardiff." Charming!

As I said though, being black at away games wasn't always a negative experience, despite travelling a lot to away matches during the era of National Front marches and attacks on minority communities, and the endless throwing of bananas and monkey chants aimed at black players. For example, there was one away game I attended where being black saved my skin from an almost certain assault.

The game in question was at Oldham's Boundary Park ground, a game I'd gone to watch with a workmate and good friend, Kevin Petty (RIP). I was 16 years old and hadn't long left school, having gone straight into an apprenticeship as an aircraft fitter with the Ministry of Defence, and had met Kevin at Barry College in the first year of a four-year apprenticeship. Kevin was the only other City fan amongst around a hundred or so apprentices with a dozen or so firms.

As he was from the area we opted to travel on a coach from Barry. The advantage of travelling with the Barry coach was that it was often the first coach to arrive at away matches. That said, I almost never made it onto the coach, as one of the older lads took exception to a young black kid joining them. Kevin was having none of it and stood up for me, offering to fight the bloke there and then. However, it soon became obvious that the objector was in a minority of one. Others interjected and welcomed me onboard.

The coach arrived at least an hour ahead of any other organised transport from Cardiff and, on finding little to do, a majority decision was taken to find the nearest pub and wait for other City fans to appear.

Although I have little recollection of the pub itself, I do remember it being full of quite large Irish labourers at the time, obviously enjoying a Saturday drink after a hard week's work. Nothing seemed untoward with the jovial banter exchanged between the Welsh and Irish. As for Kevin and me, we sat outside in the sunshine talking about the game ahead and all seemed pleasant. However, as with most away trips at the time, the peaceful and sedate atmosphere that had existed soon disappeared.

One of the lads inside the pub had had enough of the pleasantries between the Welsh and the Irish and decided to start a fight. Not exactly a good move, considering the size of the men he'd challenged, but I guess alcohol has that effect on some. Kevin and I could hear the commotion inside the pub but decided to stay outside in the sunshine. It wasn't long, however, before events took a turn for the worse.

The pub's large windows had become a target for those outside who wanted some of the action but didn't fancy getting battered by the labourers who, in fairness, despite being the victims of the attack and having fewer numbers, relished the opportunity to show their mettle. As the windows shattered, bloodied Cardiff fans could be seen inside conducting wave after wave of futile attacks, only to be repelled by much larger and much stronger opponents. Indeed, it was a completely useless endeavour to try to win a fight against men that had no interest whatsoever in football but had obviously scrapped most of their lives.

As events came to a head, out of the doorway came a large black man waving a crowbar above his head and swinging it at anyone in his path. In fact, such was the success he was having, combined by now with the Irishmen, that Cardiff fans took to their feet and ran up the road towards Boundary Park. I'd like to say that I held back ready to do my bit, offering leadership and courage, but I legged it too. Personal survival far outweighed any notion of machismo.

Not being very fit, Kevin and the other fans had built up quite a lead ahead of me and, before long, I was a good twenty or thirty yards behind them. The crowbar swinging black man was getting closer and closer, and I feared the worse. I cowered as I heard his footsteps approaching behind me, convinced that a blow to the head was imminent. As he got closer to me, Kevin stopped running to beckon me on. With this, the crowbar wielding attacker ran straight past me and gave him an almighty whack to his head. I feared the worse for Kevin, but thankfully he was made of sterner stuff and had deflected the blow with his hand.

Satisfied that his job was done, the crowbar swinger turned to walk back. This meant, of course, that I stood in his path, the only Cardiff fan between him and his mates in the pub. I cowered as he approached, convinced he would attack me next but he just laughed. "Get up mate," he said, offering me a hand, "I'm not going to attack one of my own, am I!" Kevin stood, nursing his injured hand in total disbelief, watching his attacker wish me a good day. I'm not sure he ever got over that.

Talking of away games with Kevin, it was around the

time of the Oldham match that I remember attending my first south Wales derby.

Rather than the Barry coach, we decided on catching the special football train from Cardiff Central to Swansea that had been organised for the event by the club and British Rail. The train was jam-packed, possibly a thousand or more fans eagerly anticipating the match with a lot of them trying to drink as much alcohol as was physically possible for such a short journey. It was probably because of the alcohol intake that the train took an age to get to our destination. In the main, this was due to the emergency chord being pulled at regular intervals. Indeed, such was the delay caused by the drunken antics of a few, that police officers boarded at Bridgend and had to be put into each carriage to put a stop to it. I guess it was also to stop the rest of us, who were pretty irate by then, from either lynching them or taking direct action and throwing the culprits out onto the tracks.

When the train eventually arrived in Swansea, we were rounded up and given two options: either board a fleet of double-decker buses put on for us by the local police to ferry us to the Vetch Field or be put back on a train and sent home. It wasn't the preferred option for most of the Cardiff fans at the train station that day but one which I was grateful to have been offered. Having heard all kinds of stories of ambushes and attacks in the side streets surrounding Swansea's ground, I was happy for any protection. If I'm honest, I only really went because Kevin dared me to. Anyway, I'm sure if the police had known the amount of damage that was likely to happen to the buses, they wouldn't have bothered. By the time we reached the

Vetch, I must have been one of the few that still had a seat. Most of them had been hurled out of the windows, aimed at anyone within firing distance foolish enough to taunt the buses, and a lot of these adapted projectiles had scored direct hits. Mind you, those throwing didn't seem bothered if their targets had insulted them or not, with a number of unsuspecting pensioners and shoppers, oblivious to the fact that their local team was playing its fiercest rival, taking more than their fair share of strikes.

At the ground the atmosphere was electric, and volatile. In fact, such was the tension and buzz of expectation in the queue outside, that patience to get in was wearing thin. Everybody was eager to enter the ground and a sudden roar from the masses inside caused mayhem outside. A large proportion charged at the pitiful turnstiles that stood in their way and stormed in. As they spilled through, there was little that the stewards could do. Rather than cause a riot, the only sensible thing they could do was let the remaining Cardiff fans in free of charge, me included.

As I remember, we were placed behind one of the goals in the lower section of a two-tier stand with Swansea fans directly above us. To our right was a Grandstand and to our left the long North Bank terrace crammed with Swansea fans – or so I thought until I spotted a few old school pals in with them. In fact, the more I looked, the more I noticed people I knew from Grangetown and the Docks. On further inspection, there must have been at least a couple of hundred Cardiff fans in there.

I beckoned to Kevin to look. At that very moment, all hell broke loose. The Cardiff fans on Swansea's North

Bank had decided to make their presence felt. "Kay Ar Diff!" they chanted in unison. The Swansea fans closest to them panicked and tried in vain to run in the opposite direction, tripping over each other in the process, with some spilling over the perimeter fence in abject terror. I didn't blame them. Knowing some of the Cardiff fans in there, particularly the lads from my own neck of the woods, I would have run too. Once a safe distance away, however, they soon realised that they vastly outnumbered the Cardiff fans and regrouped. For about five minutes or so, the scene resembled a *Keystone Kops* comedy, each set of fans chasing the other back and forth, exchanging punches and kicks, and beckoning their opponents on for more. Eventually, the police managed to get between them and restore order. Nevertheless, minor scuffles broke out all over the place, including the away end where a few brave Swansea souls had chanced their luck.

I also remember one chap, a rather elderly gentleman wearing half-moon glasses, taking pleasure in leaning over the tier above us from time to time to wave his Swansea scarf, laughing aloud as irate Cardiff fans tried in vain to grab at it. With each wave of the scarf, he grew more and more daring, at one point almost toppling into the away fans himself. Continuing his taunting, he leaned ever more precariously over the upper tier but the half-moon glasses that were carefully balanced on the tip of his nose fell off. They were caught by a ginger-haired Cardiff fan standing a few yards from me. The old man smiled innocently and motioned to the Cardiff fan to return them. "Sure!" shouted Ginger back at him, "No problem!" He made to throw the glasses back then changed his mind, throwing them to the floor instead before stamping his foot onto the lenses. Picking up the remains, he then bent the battered frame beyond recognition and tossed them to the tier above. "No need to thank me!" he shouted to howls of laughter.

With so much happening on the terraces, the game had completely passed me by. I had barely watched more than ten minutes of it. As it happened, we lost 2–1. In all honesty though, as much as I hate losing to Swansea, the scoreline was of little concern. More important to me was self-preservation, even more so after exiting the Vetch and seeing that the buses which had taken us there from the train station had disappeared. I should have realised that the damage done on the way to the ground would have put paid to any hope of a return service. I guess the only way I could describe my feelings at that precise moment was to say that I was well and truly bricking it. Ahead of us was a long and precarious walk to the train station, minus a police escort who, thanks to scuffles all over the place, were preoccupied to say the least. With no idea where we were or how to get to the train station, Kevin and I joined a group of older lads and hoped for the best. It's fair to say that I stuck to Kevin, who towered a good six inches over me, like glue and I don't think I've ever been so relieved to see a train station. Of course, when I got back to Cardiff I recalled tales of getting stuck in to groups of Swansea fans and running them ragged on their own patch. The truth, however, was that I couldn't wait to get out of there. I promised myself that I'd never go on a special train ever again, and to this day I still haven't.

CHAPTER 10

Depending on age, most Cardiff fans consider either Bristol City or Swansea to be the club's main rivals. A few, for some reason, think Newport County are more of a local rival while others have a thing about Bristol Rovers, or possibly Swindon or even Hereford. I suppose it's an age-related thing and wholly dependent on when you started watching the team. For me, as a teenager, the fiercest matches were always against Bristol City. I guess it was down to the fact that we hardly ever played Swansea, and while Swindon and Hereford were great away days, the corresponding matches at Ninian Park were nothing to write home about. Cardiff and Bristol were big cities and thus it was natural to view the Severnside derby as the biggest game of the season, even more so because we hardly ever used to beat Bristol City. Actually, let me correct that, we never used to beat Bristol City!

As an announcer I looked forward with relish to my first Bluebirds versus Robins match, desperately hoping that our fortunes would finally change and eager to do my bit to help bring about a positive result for the team.

We hadn't played Bristol City since the 1990s and Bristol had sold out their allocation of nearly two thousand tickets. Before the start of the game Sam Hammam took everyone by surprise by strolling into the away section of the Grange End to shake hands with some of them. Thankfully, there weren't that many Bristol fans in there at the time, however, they were still shocked by his sudden decision to join them, as were most of the security staff who had been keeping an eye on him – but that was Sam all over. He loved doing the unexpected. We should have expected it really. Nevertheless, it seemed to endear him to the visiting fans who applauded his attempt to bond with them.

Unfortunately, as the away section began to fill, what seemed like a good atmosphere soon disappeared. Jovial banter quickly turned to sheer, unadulterated hatred. Both sets of fans went on the offensive, desperately trying to out-sing each other while throwing coins, bottles and anything else they could lay their hands on. At one point, I saw what looked like a large plastic bottle of beer being tossed between rival fans, spraying quite a few as it passed back and forth over their heads. A steward later pointed out that the bottle in question had actually contained urine. Nice!

To compound matters, it was clear that some just didn't get my attempts to inject a bit of humour to proceedings, in particular Bristol's chairman who, oddly, angered at hearing songs by the Wurzels played over the tannoy, aired his contempt to Sam in the director's box. In fact, he later complained to the League about it, which beggared belief because, at the return fixture at Ashton Gate, performing live on the pitch in front of the stand housing the Cardiff fans were the Wurzels themselves! That said, they didn't stay for long, not with two thousand Cardiff fans drowning out their rendition of 'I am a cider drinker' with a collective chant of, "you're sh★t and you know you are!"

The game at Ninian Park ended in much the same way that all games involving Cardiff and Bristol had since my early years supporting the club, that is, in another defeat for

Ali with Mark Page, the Middlesbrough announcer, before our FA Cup quarter-final at the Riverside Stadium

On the pitch after our FA Cup win at Middlesbrough

Photo: Peter Thomas

The new PA room at Cardiff City Stadium

Photo: Peter Thomas

Ali with Katherine Jenkins at Wembley

Photo: Peter Thomas

FA Cup final with Half-time Wayne and Bartley the Bluebird

Portsmouth's announcer tries to 'out flag' Ali at Wembley

Wales flag at Wembley (the one Joe Ledley threw to the fans)

Photo: Peter Thomas

Claims of probe into City announcer...

HAMMERED

CARDIFF City's chief executive has launched a stinging attack on the London press over what he sees as a lying campaign against the club.

The Bluebirds have come under fire twice in recent days – first over claims that they are almost £40m in debt, which the club denies, and then that their match announcer ridiculed West Ham United fans.

But the allegations – published in a national newspaper yesterday – have not even been reported to football's governing bodies.

In the Sun, announcer Ali Yassine is accused of antagonising Hammers fans during their match against the Bluebirds on Tuesday by playing "a series of mickey-taking records" before asking for "the

Mark Stead
mark.stead@wme.co.uk

owner of a shire horse and rag and bone cart to return to his vehicle immediately." City then thrashed the East Enders 4-1 at Ninian Park.

City chief executive David Temme is furious at the way the club is being portrayed.

"We haven't heard anything and we do not expect to hear anything about this report," he said.

"One of the favourite pastimes of the London press seems to be to have a kick and a swipe at Cardiff City whenever they can.

"Why people do this, I don't know, but you can let it go over your head 99 times out of 100.

"We'll just do our talking on the pitch."

City's PA announcer Ali Yassine said he had spoken to both City owner Sam Hammam and West Ham since the game and described the reports as laughable.

"I played things like the theme tune from Steptoe & Son and My Old Man's A Dustman by Lonnie Donegan and it was all taken in good humour by everybody," he said.

"The person who wrote this report obviously hated his team being stuffed by City."

The Football Association of Wales confirmed they would have been made aware of any such complaint and none had been made.

■ City's stars of the future: See Echo Sport.

■ **HAMMER BLOW** Announcer Ali Yassine is accused of antagonising West Ham fans.

■ **ANY OLD IRONS?** The theme to Steptoe & Son was played during the visit of Londoners West Ham.

The *Sun* newspaper tries to get Ali banned

PA joker in clear

By PAUL JIGGINS

CARDIFF will not discipline their PA announcer for taking the mic out of West Ham fans.

Ali Yasfem poked fun at the 700 Hammers supporters at Ninian Park on Tuesday by playing songs such as London Bridge Is Falling Down, My Old Man's A Dustman and the theme from Steptoe and Son.

He then asked "for the owner of a horse attached to a rag and bone cart in the visitors' car park to return to his vehicle immediately."

But a Cardiff spokesman said: "We will not be taking any action. It was just a bit of fun and we don't believe it upset anybody.

"In fact, the West Ham directors at the game said Ali made their evening."

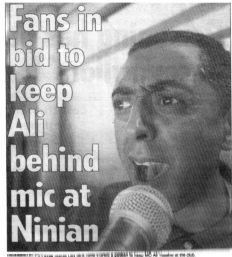

Gareth Rogers

ANGRY Cardiff City fans started a petition to reinstate popular matchday announcer Ali Yassine, after fears he was facing the boot.

Fans voiced concern that the

Announcer 'could work with new DJs' – City spokesman

The *Sun* admits defeat   *South Wales Echo* article: fans bid to keep Ali

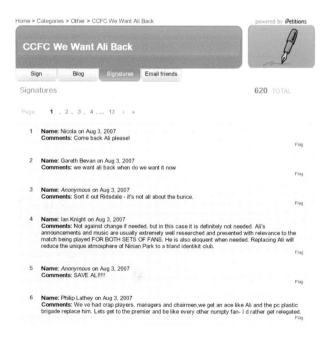

CCFC We Want Ali Back

Sign   Blog   Signatures   Email friends

Signatures   **620** TOTAL

Page: **1** , 2 , 3 , 4 ,... 13 › »

1   **Name:** Nicola on Aug 3, 2007
Comments: Come back Ali please!
    Flag

2   **Name:** Gareth Bevan on Aug 3, 2007
Comments: we want ali back when do we want it now
    Flag

3   **Name:** Anonymous on Aug 3, 2007
Comments: Sort it out Ridsdale - it's not all about the bunce.
    Flag

4   **Name:** Ian Knight on Aug 3, 2007
Comments: Not against change if needed, but in this case it is definitely not needed. Ali's announcements and music are usually extremely well researched and presented with relevance to the match being played FOR BOTH SETS OF FANS. He is also eloquent when needed. Replacing Ali will reduce the unique atmosphere of Ninian Park to a bland identikit club.
    Flag

5   **Name:** Anonymous on Aug 3, 2007
Comments: SAVE ALI!!!!!
    Flag

6   **Name:** Philip Lathey on Aug 3, 2007
Comments: We ve had crap players, managers and chairmen,we get an ace like Ali and the pc plastic brigade replace him. Lets get to the premier and be like every other numpty fan- I d rather get relegated.
    Flag

Fans sign an online petition to keep Ali at Ninian Park

Ali exchanges shirts with Reading announcer, Paul Allen

Photo: Peter Thomas

Ali, Half-time Wayne, Jasper and Bartley at Ninian Park

Photo: Peter Thomas

Ali doing the Ayatollah at Ninian Park

South Wales Echo
feature

Announcer Ali explains why he's got the best job in the world

■ Ninian announcer Ali Yassine has been with the club since 2001

As Bluebirds' fans say goodbye to Ninian Park, *Tim Lewis* speaks to some of the people who have made it so memorable

ALI YASSINE, stadium announcer, has been with the club since 2001 shortly after Sam Hammam took control.

He said: "I've got the best job in the world. I have a lot of freedom to do what I want, I get a great seat and I get to have a laugh with the fans. The best part of the job is probably announcing the name of the scorer who's just scored the winner, I take a lot of pleasure from that and it still feels great every time."

Ali has become well known in football, not just with Cardiff fans, and spends hours preparing for his job in the days leading up to a game.

He's probably the only football team announcer in the league with his own catchphrase. But did you know that Ali Yassine has acted, presented and he's soon to direct four episodes of EastEnders! **Jo Manning** went to meet him.

Making some noise

Western Mail feature

the Bluebirds, and this despite taking the lead. The return match, although not as depressing for Cardiff fans, proved slightly better with a 1–1 draw.

★

In the season that followed I knew that I'd be told to tone everything down for the Severnside derby, however, the game at Ninian Park had given me an idea. I guess, having not played Bristol in a while, it should have come as no surprise that a lot of the older heads, some who hadn't been to watch the team in many a season, had gone along to reminisce about past encounters and with them came a few of the old chants. Hearing the chants got me thinking about their origins, in other words, the songs, mostly pop songs at that, that were the original source of many of them. Some were easy to work out. For example, as a young lad, a terrace favourite for me had been Cliff Richard's 1960s hit 'Bachelor Boy', whose chorus had been changed from 'son you are a bachelor boy' to 'son you are a Cardiff fan'. A more recent chant was taken from the Dubliners' song, 'Lord of the Dance', whose chorus had been transformed from 'dance dance, wherever you may be… ' to 'fight, fight, wherever you may be, we ★★★★★★★ hate the West Country'. Another hit for quite a number of singers was 'You are my sunshine', which became 'You are my Cardiff' and Lee Marvin's lyrics from 'Wandering Star', a number one single from the film *Paint Your Wagon*, changed from 'I was born under a wandering star' to 'I was born under a Grange End star'. In fairness, many had stood the test of time and were equally as popular years later. Others, however, had not and were difficult to track down having originated from obscure 1950s or 1960s chart songs such as Jim Reeves' 'Distant Drums'. With more and more vocal away fans coming to Ninian Park, the words had been rearranged to:

> *I hear the sound of distant bums*
> *Over there, over there*
> *And do they smell*
> *Like f****** hell!*

'Side by side', a song originally released in 1927 by Harry Woods, was another turned into a terrace chant and became a skinhead classic in the 1970s:

> *Oh, we ain't got a lot of manners.*
> *We fight with razors and spanners (or sometimes hammers),*
> *We are the skins, in Doctor Martins, side by side.*

Max Bygraves' 'Teddy Bears' Picnic' was another skinhead favourite and became:

> *If you go down to the woods today*
> *You're sure of a big surprise.*
> *If you go down to the woods today*
> *You'd better go in disguise!*
> *For Jeremy the Sugar Puff bear*
> *Has bought some boots and cropped his hair*
> *Jeremy the Sugar Puff's joined the Skinheads.*

Another favourite of the skinheads, a surprising choice too, was 'Tiptoe through the tulips', a song originally published in 1929, revived in 1967 by the California rock group The Humane Society and again in 1968 by Tiny

Tim, whose high-pitched version charted at number 17 that year. The verse, by the time it reached Ninian Park, had become:

> *Tiptoe through the Grange End with me flick knife and me*
> *   hobnail boots.*
> *Come tiptoe through the Grange End with me.*

I played as many of the original songs as I could find. I mean, how could I possibly get into trouble for playing middle-of-the-road songs from yesteryear? Thankfully, nobody from within the club had picked up on it. On the other hand, friends of mine certainly did, judging by the amount of text messages I was getting on the day of the Bristol match. Most were laughing and singing along, much to the bemusement of the younger fans around them, however, it made little difference to the score. We lost, again. Worse still, a Cardiff boy, and a City fan to boot, Christian Roberts, had scored the second goal of a 2–0 defeat to put the match beyond reach, much to the delight of the visiting fans. In fairness to him, Christian refused to celebrate the goal. In fact, he looked as disappointed as the rest of the Cardiff fans that day. Would we ever beat Bristol bloody City?

As luck would have it, the Bluebirds made it into the League One play-offs again. However, such was our misfortune, we got the only team we'd never beaten in my lifetime of supporting the team. Yes, Bristol bloody City! Indeed, after the heartache of losing to Stoke the previous season, promotion to the Championship now seemed an even more distant dream.

By the time the game came around, I'd fallen out with the club's Chief Executive, David Temme (RIP), and decided to quit. It was a shame really because I liked David. He'd had his moments with the Cardiff City fans, as do all chief execs and owners from time to time, but was a decent bloke nonetheless. In fact, I can barely remember why we fell out. As I recall, he'd asked me to attend a meeting where he was giving a few members of staff the 'hair-dryer treatment' over something or other and, much to his amazement, I walked out. When he later sought me out, angered at such disregard for his authority, I told him that I worked for Cardiff City as an escape from my day job. The last thing I needed was being lectured for following Sam's wishes i.e. winding up the opposition. David gave me an ultimatum – obey or go. Regretfully, I went.

In a way, however, I preferred being back on the terrace with my mates for the play-off semi-final. For one thing, I'd missed being on the Grange End and particularly missed the feeling of belonging that came with years of watching the Bluebirds with the same crowd. I didn't know half the names of the people surrounding me but they were familiar faces all the same. These were the people I felt most at home with. In fact, I still don't know the names of the majority of them but that is the beauty of football. It doesn't matter. In saying that, I almost missed the game after a couple of stewards, convinced for some reason that I was up to no good, tried to eject me from the ground. I guess all the insults aimed at them over the tannoy had put paid to any goodwill. Thankfully though, friends rallied around to refute their accusations.

The noise and tension inside Ninian Park was incredible

with over 19,000 fans there, and having completed the double over us that season, it was obvious that Bristol's players and fans were in confident mood – over-confident if anything.

It had to happen though, and it did. For the first time since 1971, we actually beat them. A single solitary goal was all that stood between us that day and, surprisingly, it's one of the few goals I ever remember, scored by Peter Thorne in the 74th minute. I don't think I'd ever seen so many happy people at a football game. Not only finally beating one of our fiercest rivals but taking an advantage, a single precious goal, into the second leg. More than anything, it gave us real hope after our capitulation against Stoke. Surely they couldn't cock it up this time.

I didn't go the second leg of the semi at Ashton Gate. I was too nervous. I should have gone though, as I was probably just as anxious, if not more, listening to the game on the radio at a friend's house. Actually, it was the same friend, Paul Skagestad, with who I had attended my first-ever game. We spent the entire match in almost complete silence, our hearts skipping a beat, heads buried in hands, every time Bristol attacked. In fact I could barely sit for most of the commentary, pacing up and down the room, wearing my footprints into his carpet and pleading for the final whistle. At the end, I don't think I have ever celebrated a goalless draw in the same way. I stood with my arms raised aloft letting out a scream of joy that could probably be heard in Bristol, while my friend just punched the air in silent celebration. We danced, skipped around his living room, pulled funny faces at each other and generally made ourselves look like complete idiots to anyone passing his window. Indeed, it was only when I left that I realised that his curtains had been open all night, but it didn't matter. The Bluebirds had reached a play-off final and it would be right here in the city's Millennium Stadium. Cardiff was going to go mental, and it did.

★

History, of course, recorded a win for the team at the final, thanks to an extra-time winner by Andy Campbell. However, as much as I enjoyed the day, I have to say that I was gutted at not being a part of the pre-match proceedings, particularly because the tannoy announcers get an invite to do a slot on the pitch. More galling was hearing someone else shouting "Support the boys and make some noise!" I guess petulance has its price. Then again, they do say that imitation is the best form of flattery. Nevertheless, it was a day that will probably never be repeated in the Bluebird's history, that is, the club winning promotion in its own city. I mean, other than London-based clubs, there can't be that many other clubs, if any at all, that could say the same. Football die-hards, naturally, insist that Wembley is the real home of football and that the Millennium Stadium is really a rugby stadium, and having been to Wembley, it's difficult to argue with them. All the same, the Millennium Stadium is an amazing arena and that final was scripted for Cardiff to win. I did feel a little sorry for the other finalists, Queens Park Rangers, whose fans took defeat very well, but it was a turning point in our history and one to savour at that.

CHAPTER 11

Being back on the terrace for the League One play-off semi-final had reminded me of how much I enjoyed the amount and variety of chants that Cardiff fans usually conjure up on a match day – often responding to the action on and off the pitch. I suppose it's the variety of chants heard at football grounds up and down the country which makes football so appealing to a lot of my generation, and it's something that excites youngsters on their first visit. Also, a visit from Cardiff was rarely a quiet affair and would often give other teams' fans a chance to scream and shout on a national 'England versus Wales' level.

I'm not really into chants that are downright nasty; however, there have been quite a few that have given me a laugh over the years. Some of my favourites have included:

> *Robbie Fowler's magic, he's got a cracking shot.*
> *And when he signed for Cardiff, he said, "I'm buying Splott".*
> *He bought up half the Valleys and all the Gurnos too.*
> *And forty thousand Bluebirds said, "I'm gonna live with you".*
> (to the tune of 'My old man's a dustman')

> *Fan Zhiyi is magic*
> *He wears a magic hat*
> *And when he came to Cardiff*
> *He said, "I Fan Zhiyi that".*

Alan Cork, Alan Cork, Alan, Alan Cork
He's got no hair
But we don't care
Alan, Alan Cork.

When the boss says he'll stay,
Then he's gone the next day,
That's Roberto (Martinez).
(to the tune of 'That's Amore')

His name is Gerrard,
Anthony Gerrard,
He's got a cousin called Stevie G.
But now young Tony is much more famous,
Because he's signed for Cardiff City!

Who needs Cantona when we've got Stantona!

Lee, Lee Bowyer!
We wanna know why you're not in jail!
(to the tune of 'Hey Baby')

Dimi, Dimi, Dimi, Dimi, Dimi, Konstantopoulos.
He swam away, to Cardiff Bay.
(to the tune of 'Karma Chameleon')

Who put the ball in the English net?
Arfur, Arfur?
Who put the ball in the English net?
Arfur f****** Europe!

He plays on the left
He plays on the right
That boy Chris Burke
Makes Routledge look sh★te!
(to the tune of 'Sloop John B')

The wheels on your house go round and round,
Round and round, round and round
The wheels on your house go round and round,
All day long…
(to the tune of 'Wheels on the Bus')

Feed the Jacks, let them know it's Christmas time!
(to the tune of 'Feed the World')

He's not even Welsh
He's not even Welsh
That Ashley Williams
He's not even Welsh
(to the tune of 'Sloop John B')

Oh Kev McNaughton, you are the love of my life
Oh Kev McNaughton, I'll let you sh★g my wife,
Oh Kev McNaughton, I want silver hair too!
(to the tune of 'Can't Take my Eyes off of You')

CHAPTER 12

As time went by, there was no stopping Sam Hammam. Mind you, I don't think anyone's ever had the nerve to try stopping Sam. If he had his mind set on something, there was nothing anyone could do to change it, and Cardiff City was no exception. In fact, it hadn't taken long before the club had completely adopted his personality, whether it was getting apprentices to let down the tyres of the first team squad's cars or the serving of sheep's testicles as part of a Ninian Park buffet – one thing was certain – with Sam around, life at the football club was never dull. Others, of course, felt completely different towards him. I don't think some of the staff ever got him. Mind you, he used to sack quite a few of them on a daily basis, often reinstating them as they made to go with a few choice words like, "Baby, where are you going?"

Sam was definitely one of those 'marmite' people. You either loved him or hated him. There certainly weren't many who were indifferent to him. Some away fans loved him but most hated Sam, especially if he did his customary walk around the pitch prior to kick-off. Indeed, the regularity of away fans pelting him with objects meant that he needed the protection of his own bodyguard. In fact, when Leeds came to town an infamous FA Cup match in 2002, as well as enough coins to fill a piggy bank, the ground staff later cleared the pitch of bottles, lighters, mobile phones, a belt and a solitary shoe. Thankfully, I've only ever been overly emotional at a game once. This was as a teenager at an away game in Wrexham when a quite brilliant save caused me to toss a cold beef and onion pie in the direction of goalkeeper Dai Davies. However, much like my footballing skills, it missed its target and landed harmlessly behind his goal.

Cardiff fans, on the whole, loved Sam, especially when he first came to the club. More than anything, he made supporting the Bluebirds exciting again. On top of that, Sam was accessible to fans and thrived on forming a good relationship with supporters through organised meet and greets all over south Wales, even in Swansea. I remember going to a few of these get-togethers in Cardiff and the Valleys. In saying that, I don't think I was ever invited – I generally used to gatecrash the events. It was usually the hottest ticket in town, drawing huge crowds wherever Sam went. He was certainly an infectious person, easily engaging his audience whether they were supportive or critical. However, giving Sam a microphone was often tantamount to throwing petrol on a fire. He hardly ever held back and his choice of language, although inspirational, was usually pretty colourful, to say the least. They were certainly not words for the faint-hearted.

Sharing Arab roots with Sam gave me a different perspective on him, but it also meant that my relationship with him was altogether different from most. In Arab culture, respect for your elders is paramount to everything, particularly your parents and even more so your grandparents. You never disrespect or question their motives; you just do what they say. Yet Sam was also like the best boss I could ever wish for, always supportive and always positive about the future of the club, and my role in it.

Sam's 'crazy gang' spirit, a mindset that had become famous at Wimbledon, was transferred to Cardiff City, and the tannoy was just another way of getting the message across to the masses. If truth be told, from time to time, Sam would take a hands-on approach and wander into Ninian Park's cramped PA box, sitting himself next to me and say, "Ali baby, it's St George's Day. Let's wind the English up!"

One thing I loved about Sam was the importance he attached to family, not just his own but to everyone connected with Cardiff City. If you were a Cardiff fan, you were a part of his family. Furthermore, he encouraged many of us to bring along our partners and children to games as well as other club functions. Indeed, he often tried to get me to bring my parents along to matches and would regularly ask about their well-being.

Sam also loved being around children who came to Ninian Park, whether on a match day or not. I'll never forget watching him challenge two of my daughters to a race on the Ninian Park pitch before a league game. Despite my protestations, they were happy to oblige, thinking it would be an easy win. However, I don't think they realised that Sam would take it so seriously. Mind you, considering his heart problems, I was a bit apprehensive of Sam, a man in his sixties, taking on a ten year-old and a twelve year-old in a fifty-metre sprint. As it happened, he beat them hands down although, to this day, they claim that they never really tried to win.

I can honestly say that I miss Sam Hammam's days at the club. They were never dull and although the club has moved on, the crazy antics helped create a sense of fun about the place, a sense of fun that, although not so obvious these days, is still there. It also meant that I could get away with almost anything. There was no way Sam would sack someone he deemed as crazy as himself.

CHAPTER 13

Ever since learning to speak Welsh at the age of 25 and going on to work in the Welsh-language television and radio industry, I've often worked with Swansea fans. In fact, I once had the distinguished honour of joining one of them, Ian Walsh, along with Wrexham fan, Ian Gwyn Hughes, in their commentary position high above the North Bank for a local derby. This was when Cardiff fans had been banned from the Vetch. Both Ians had warned me not to react to anything on the pitch, as the home fans had been known to throw objects up to the commentary position on the gantry or, at worst, to try climbing the ladder to vent their frustration in person. I was actually surprised to see how many had radios glued to their ears and they were certainly quick with their expletives when they disagreed with the commentators. I joined in at one point, however, miming 'Ian Walsh, you're a w★★★★★!' while he tried to give his views on the match.

I'd go as far as to say that I've had a real laugh working with a lot of jacks. Unfortunately, however, most of the people from Swansea I've worked with prefer rugby to football, which makes the relationship I've had with genuine Swans fans a bit more special. In all honesty, the banter between the clubs is so much better when you actually know a few, especially in this modern era of texting. Also, they are easy to wind up and nothing frustrates Swansea workmates more than stating that Cardiff's main local rival is Bristol City. It might have been true years ago, but most Cardiff fans agree that beating Swansea is much sweeter than beating Bristol City these days. It's a great excuse whenever they beat us though.

A lot of Cardiff fans don't know that I'm actually on good terms with my counterparts at Swansea, particularly Kevin Johns, their main announcer and club padre, and their Welsh-speaking announcer, Eirian Wyn. Despite his position as the club's religious leader, such is the banter between us that whenever I speak to Kevin on the phone, he often addresses me as 'scummer'. When it comes to football though, Kevin and I have a similar sense of humour. More than anything, we accept that we both love our clubs as much as the other. We also share the belief that fans make the game what it is and, therefore, should be given a day to remember, on and off the pitch. After all, without fans and the rivalries, and without the atmosphere generated by both home and away supporters, the game itself has little meaning.

I first spoke to Kevin just before my first south Wales derby as a tannoy announcer, preparing the ground for what was likely to be a volatile atmosphere and looking for ideas in which to use laughter to diffuse any likely conflict between the fans. In saying that, I didn't tell him, or should I say, I 'forgot' to tell him, that I'd got some cheap laughs at Ninian Park a few weeks earlier at Swansea's expense by announcing to a packed stadium that their former chairman, Tony Petty, a man still despised by Swans fans for putting their club's very existence in jeopardy, had sent me a good luck card wishing Cardiff well against them in the upcoming FAW Premier Cup final, emphasising the point by declaring that he had "done his bit, now you do yours!" I hadn't told Kevin either that I'd 'allegedly' referred to their new stadium as a Caravan Park whilst apologising to any members of the travelling community for associating them with Swansea. Anyway, it was only a bit of leg-pulling.

Nevertheless, having been given the green light by Kevin, I set about putting a playlist together that might give both sets of fans a laugh, whatever the final outcome. It's worth pointing out though that I had two playlists ready for that evening. The first was a bog-standard middle-of-the-road playlist consisting mainly of chart music, whilst the second was an altogether different affair, aimed at having as much fun at Swansea's expense as possible. I guess the reason for this was because of Cardiff's promotion demise from the League One play-offs at the hands of Stoke City in the semi-final. I also had a sneaking suspicion that Swansea's 1,500 visiting fans, given free buses at the time by Sam Hammam in a bid to end the bitterness, would use the FAW Cup final as an opportunity to have fun at our expense – a no-brainer really.

More in a state of hope than anything else, I started the night with the mediocre playlist, probably still a bit shell-shocked, like everyone else at the club – fans and staff alike – about the Stoke result.

I should have known better. No sooner had the first of the Swansea buses arrived, out came the England and Union Jack flags with Stoke emblazoned on them and chants of, "You're not going up, you're not going up, you're not going, you're not going, you're not going up!"

The game itself was nothing to write home about, quite a dire affair really, but as half-time approached, the first playlist went in the bin and out came the alternative version. As the players traipsed off at the end of the first half, I pressed play on the CD player. Cher's 'Gypsies, tramps, and thieves' blasted over the tannoy, cheered on by the Cardiff faithful who'd got the joke straight away and sang along.

Half-times are always busy affairs what with birthday announcements, sponsor notices and half-time scores to read out, as well as writing last minute messages, downloading scores or working out timings in order to get all the corporate stuff out in the allotted time. It often means that I never get to enjoy them. However, that night's affair was completely different, even more so because I hadn't expected the reaction the half-time 'alternative' playlist would get. Indeed, one of the fans sat in front of the tannoy box gave the window a bang to get my attention and beckoned me out to see. As I poked my head out of the door, to the side of me, almost the entire stand were on their feet, waving ten and twenty pound notes at the Swansea fans, and singing along to Simply Red's 'Money's too tight to mention'.

The game continued but never quite lived up to expectations, even though we took the lead through an exquisitely placed Graham Kavanagh free kick and finished winning 1–0. I suppose it helped take a little bit of the sting out of the Stoke game, especially beating a local rival, but in reality it was, as often described in those situation, a meaningless Mickey Mouse cup game.

I didn't hear from Kevin for quite a while after that. I guess losing to your local rival hurts Swansea fans as well. However, having suggested to the Football Association of Wales that it might be a good idea to use us both for Wales games, we soon got together again at the Millennium

Stadium – myself on the microphone for most of the game with Kevin doing a stint at half-time. Indeed, his background as a radio presenter and part-time pantomime performer made him perfect for the role.

As for future south Wales derby games, their volatility meant a complete toning down of activities on the tannoy, mainly due to the continued troubles between certain sections of the support. The odd laugh was acceptable but, on the whole, a new approach had to be taken. In saying that, I still get quite a number of requests for 'Gypsies, tramps, and thieves' every time we play them. That said, Kevin and Eirian apart, officials and staff at Swansea have never forgiven me for playing Cher or referring to their stadium as a Caravan Park. This, despite the continual jibes about Cardiff from them, whether it's a dig at our finances or poking fun at our new stadium, tagged 'Legoland' by the Swans faithful.

I remember on one occasion I was working for the Welsh FA at the Liberty Stadium and, as well as wearing an official tracksuit and possessing every pass imaginable – giving me access to every part of the ground, from the tunnel and pitch to the PA room and public areas – my every move was scrutinised. No matter where I went I was stopped and forced to show some means of identification. The pettiness was extreme to say the least. Not only were passes hanging from my neck, each was checked again and again for authenticity. Such was the level of interrogation that accompanied this never-ending ritual that a number of FAW staff were taken aback by the methods adopted by the staff at the Liberty in order to make my visit uncomfortable. Welcome I was certainly not. At first, I found the whole affair quite amusing. There I was, so obviously working for the FAW, constantly singled out and having to prove my identity, and often by the same security staff. After the fifth or sixth time it began to get a bit tedious. The FAW's chief, David Collins, on the other hand, didn't take too kindly to a member of his staff being treated in such a manner and had it stopped immediately, much to the annoyance of Swansea's stewards.

I can take a little antagonism. However, sometimes the sheer hatred aimed at Cardiff by Swansea is hard to stomach. In saying that, not until I'd spent some time working in Swansea had I realised the extent of the bitterness folk out west have towards their capital city. And it isn't just football, it's everything, from the fact that Cardiff is the capital city of Wales to the location of the National Assembly and the head offices of every major corporation in the Principality – it all irks people from Swansea. They even complain about the media talking up Cardiff and the fact that Cardiff appears in the background of the Welsh news on television.

I guess the bitterness really hit home while spending almost a year working in and around the area. I was in Swansea having won a commission to film a documentary series for BBC Wales called *Away From Home*, which followed the fortunes of a team of asylum seekers called the Swansea World Stars as they aspired to change attitudes to refugees by playing football in Division Four of the Swansea Senior League. For me, this entailed commuting every other weekend and filming a number of their matches, as well as their attempts to integrate into the local community. Wherever I went, however, as soon as I opened my mouth, the inevitable words came, "you're from Cardiff, aren't you mush!" No sooner had I acknowledged my place of birth than moan after moan came about Cardiff getting everything and Swansea getting nothing.

On the whole, the banter around the matches was pretty jovial but on one or two occasions, particularly if I returned an insult or stood up for my hometown, events could just as easily take a turn for the worse. Thankfully, I was never alone and there were many sensible locals around to quell any likelihood of trouble. Also, working for the BBC meant a modicum of respect from opposing teams that wanted their clubs to be seen in a good light.

Overall, the experience enlightened me somewhat as to why people from Swansea feel so aggrieved about Cardiff and, in a way, I felt sorry for them. That said, in comparison, Cardiff is as prosperous as it is because of the calibre of people that helped and continue to help push its development. I guess it also suits some in Swansea to live in Cardiff's shadow, reaffirming their hard-done-by attitude. It's an attitude that also, although to a lesser extent, exists in Cardiff, an attitude that is very Welsh. Indeed, it's an attitude that many from smaller cities and, for that matter, smaller countries have when a larger, more prosperous neighbour holds influence over them. I guess it's an easy way out.

CHAPTER 14

Working for the Welsh FA has to go down as one of the best jobs I've ever had, especially when it involved a packed Millennium Stadium – as was often the case when Mark Hughes was manager. Not only did I have a great relationship with the staff of the FAW, I also loved the fact that they treated everybody the same, whether you were the head of the organisation or the tea lady.

After my first game, the Wales v Argentina friendly, another friendly had been arranged between Wales and Germany, featuring a German side that included players such as Bayern Munich's Oliver Khan in goal, Tottenham's Christian Ziege and Liverpool's Dietmar Hamman in midfield, and AS Monaco's Oliver Bierhoff and FC Kaiserslautern's Miroslav Klose in attack. Wales, on the other hand, included the likes of Robbie Savage, Mark Pembridge and Robert Page. Fair enough, we also had Ryan Giggs, Gary Speed and Simon Davies in the team but, on paper, nowhere near a team good enough to match our visitors. Indeed, most, particularly the English press had completely written off any hope of a draw, let alone Welsh victory.

As usual, I aimed to have as much fun with the crowd as possible and used the opportunity to practice the little German I had picked up in school and from a friend that spoke the language fluently. I looked forward to showing off my attempt at fluency and practiced with aplomb. "Ladies and gentlemen, meine damen und herren," I began, "Ich bin ein Cardiffian… innit!" This was followed by the phrase I had learned so earnestly from a German-speaking friend, "Sich vor Angst in die Hose scheiben." Unfortunately, I had no idea until after the event that I'd just told the visiting fans that we were terribly afraid of their team or, to put it bluntly, were 'shitting bricks'. I could have strangled the so-called 'friend'.

It might well have been true; however, against all the odds, Wales won the game. Indeed, the team were fearless of their opponents that evening and showed little respect for Germany's fierce reputation with Savage clattering into them at every opportunity, causing the German players to turn to the referee in disgust at their treatment. The game was capped by a fairy tale debut for Cardiff's own Robert Earnshaw, who popped up to score the winning goal twelve seconds into the second half. More than anything, it was a performance that gave the team and the fans real belief that something big could be achieved under Mark Hughes.

The atmosphere in the stadium had been incredible, so much so that at the end of the match I just couldn't help myself. I switched on the microphone and, buoyed by the win and inspired by Norwegian television commentator, Bjørge Lillelien, bellowed out an adaptation of his famous words, "Ludwig van Beethoven, Boris Becker, Albert Einstein, Michael Schumacher, Claudia Schiffer! Can you hear me Claudia Schiffer? You're boys took one hell of a beating!"

Seeing those words quoted in a few match reports the following day gave me a real buzz. In fact, later that year after a 2–1 win over Italy, a few of the papers quoted my final remarks again. "Friends, Welshmen, countrymen! Lend me your ears! Wales 2, Italy 1. Beeeeellissssimoooo!"

Like the Germany game, nobody had given Wales a cat in hell's chance of beating Italy and the win had propelled us to the top of Group 9 of the World Cup qualifiers. Who'd have thought!

Prior to the Italy game, the FAW had booked the Manic Street Preachers to play on the pitch as part of a pre-match programme of entertainment and had Bryn Terfel there to sing the national anthems. It was deemed such a success (particularly in that it meant fans could come into the stadium a good deal earlier and be entertained), that it was decided to try to stick to the same strategy for the rest of the campaign. More than anything, it helped the stadium stewards deal with the influx of a 70,000 plus crowd far easier, particularly as most fans seemed to wait until ten minutes before kick-off to make their way into the Millennium Stadium. I guess the stadium's location, smack bang in the middle of Cardiff, with pubs directly outside, generally meant that fans were happy to wander in a few minutes before kick-off.

Anyway, it fell on my shoulders, along with help from Rupert Moon, to ensure that things went smoothly, from the organising of popular bands to arranging anthem singers and half-time entertainment. From then on Welsh fans were able to sample the delights of groups such as the Super Furry Animals and Feeder to solo singers such as Mike Peters from the Alarm and Dafydd Iwan – the only criteria was that they were Welsh or had members who were Welsh.

One of the most memorable group of performers

appeared in the World Cup campaign of 2006. I had invited Goldie Lookin' Chain to showcase their music prior to a match against England in a sell-out Millennium Stadium on a hot Saturday afternoon in September 2005. I kind of knew things would be a bit different when they turned up for a sound check a couple of hours before kick-off. At the time, the stadium was empty, bar a few hundred stewards and media crews getting ready for the big game. Goldie Lookin' Chain marched onto the pitch and, as soon as their microphones were switched on, one of them yelled out at the empty stadium, "Helloooo Wembley!" Even the stadium manager laughed at that one.

Such was their popularity – there must have been at least thirty to forty thousand fans in the stadium when the time came for Goldie Lookin' Chain to perform. I guess their chart hit, 'Guns don't kill people, rappers do', and an appearance from Maggot on *Celebrity Big Brother* had a lot to do with that. However, this was still around an hour before kick-off.

The England team were warming up a few feet away from them and, looking down on them from the hospitality boxes was an array of celebrities, including Victoria Beckham. You can guess what happened next. Goldie Lookin' Chain decided to dedicate their final song, an as yet unheard new single, to David Beckham. It was called 'Your missus is a nutter'. On top of that, when the chorus came around, the group asked the entire stadium to stand up and join in, waving their arms from side to side which they did, much to the horror of Victoria Beckham who, disgusted by the collective lack of respect for her, decided to retire to her hospitality box, pronto.

As it was, David Beckham seemed to take the slight in good humour. However, the furore that followed was incredible. In the first instance, I was summoned to the FAW to face a rather angry David Collins, the FAW's Secretary General. David was livid that such disrespect had been shown to David Beckham and his wife. In addition, journalists were calling to ask for a quote and, as if to add fuel to the fire, Goldie Lookin' Chain phoned me to ask if we could ban them. After all, a ban would help sales of their new single. I told them that they could consider themselves banned from future invites, which pleased them no end. In fact, I've never had to pay for a Goldie Lookin' Chain ticket since.

All things aside, Mark Hughes' tenure brought me many happy memories. He was a very popular manager with players, staff and fans alike, and he held the belief that the fans could act as a twelfth man. Furthermore, the Welsh FA's policy of cheap tickets, combined with the fact that the Millennium Stadium still had a wow factor about it, with many attending football matches for the first time there, boded well for fantastic, fervent atmospheres in the stadium. Indeed, a giant Nationwide sponsors flag used to fly at international games with the words 'Pride, Passion and Belief' emblazoned on it, which reflected that period of time perfectly.

Alas, with regards to qualifying for a major tournament, it wasn't to be. However, I still remember being approached at the end of the final play-off game against Russia by a gentleman who asked me what my role was with the FAW. When I told him that, despite the tracksuit etc., I was merely the tannoy announcer, he replied,

"Well, let me tell you this. You had a great game!" I had no idea who he was until a colleague from the FAW asked what Eric Harrison had said. "Who?" I replied, to which he chuckled and walked off. In all honesty, I hadn't realised that Eric Harrison, the man who approached me, was Mark Hughes' assistant and mentor, and a former assistant to Alex Ferguson at Manchester United.

CHAPTER 15

Most people think that the tannoy announcer has the easiest job in the world. I mean, how difficult is it to sit in a room with a great view of the game, reading a couple of team sheets, making a few birthday announcements and playing a few songs on a CD player? Well, that was certainly the view of Bristol-based Kiss 101's DJs, whose company had offered the club a deal to take over the tannoy on match days. The offer was aimed at increasing the radio station's popularity in south Wales, but came with the condition that they placed their own people in the ground rather than Half-time Wayne and me.

It was Peter Ridsdale's first full season as chairman, having taken the reins halfway through the previous season and, I guess, on the face of it, it seemed a good deal for the club. It meant free publicity and a bit of cash. The problem, however, was that Cardiff City had its own unique identity, an identity that was treasured by its fans. After all, at the time, we were Wales' only representatives in the Championship. How much of this would Kiss 101 retain?

I'd heard a rumour that things might change for both me and Wayne, my partner in crime at Ninian Park, but hadn't realised how quickly events would take shape. The club had left it quite late in the day to tell me, so caught me off guard. I still remember the shocked reaction of some of the girls in the ticket office when I bought a season ticket, and had quite a few people approach me on the Grange End prior to our pre-season friendly against Ajax to ask what I was doing outside the PA box.

The two new announcers, Reece and Jasper, were sold as local lads who supported the club and, to be fair, they did but both also supported Premier Division clubs. In Reece's case it was Everton while Jasper was a Liverpool fan. That didn't bother me but rumbles of discontent grew when supporters made these discoveries on the lads' own website pages.

I hadn't met Jasper before but Reece was someone I'd crossed paths with earlier. Reece had taken over for one of the most important games in the club's history, a League One play-off semi-final against Bristol City. This came about after my falling out with the club's Chief Executive, David Temme, as mentioned earlier.

Because of that he was invited to the play-off final itself as the club's official announcer and given a five minute slot on the Millennium Stadium pitch to help create a bit of banter. In all honesty, I wasn't too gutted, as not going to the final in an official capacity meant I was able to enjoy the day with a group of mates that had been terrace companions at home and away matches for years. After all, and I'm sure most football fans agree, sharing your team's special moments are that much better with people who had also suffered the many disappointments with you. That said, it was still a bit weird hearing him scream out my tried and trusted line, "Support the boys and make some noise", especially when people mistook him for me. In fact, I overheard someone behind me say, "Bloody hell, I must be losing it! I could have sworn Ali was a black dude from the Docks. I hadn't realised he was a white lad from the Valleys."

After that, Reece started the Championship campaign as the club's announcer but lasted just one game before making the mistake of all mistakes by playing the England anthem 'Football's Coming Home'. The reaction was incredible. Boos rang out all around the ground and a livid Sam Hammam could be seen stomping his way to the tannoy box, exiting with the CD in hand and snapping it in half to cheers from the terraces. A few days later, I received a phone call from him demanding that I returned.

Fast-forward a few years later and there I was on the Grange End again watching City in a pre-season friendly with Reece sat in the tannoy box again – this time working for Kiss 101. The famous Dai Hunt, one of Cardiff's more vocal supporters, approached me and got those around him to chant "We want Ali back!" Dai's cause was also helped by the fact that Reece made a hash of the substitutions, mispronounced a few of the players' names and tried to get a chant of "Robbie, Robbie, Robbie" going, in reference to our new signing, Robbie Fowler, by playing the Kaiser Chief's new single 'Ruby', but to no avail. Indeed, it just made Dai even more vocal on the Grange End.

It still makes me laugh when I think back to that game. Our opponents escape me, possibly Den Haag, but I remember clearly being approached by a number of stewards who claimed that I was egging Mr Hunt on. However, anyone who knew Dai also knew that he needed no encouragement whatsoever. He's one of Cardiff City's real characters and, love him or hate him, as passionate about the club as they come.

This time the story of my departure made the local newspapers, more so because of an online petition organised by some of the fans that drew over six hundred names in a matter of days. I was gobsmacked by the support and, within a few days, was summoned to the club for a meeting with the new CEO.

I remember walking into the club's boardroom with the media manager, Julian Jenkins, and was greeted by the new chairman, Peter Ridsdale. "It seems you have lots of friends around here, Ali," he began. "It's good to have friends," I replied. "I wouldn't know about that," was his response. Fair play, despite all that had happened to him following his departure from Leeds, at least he retained a sense of humour.

Peter explained that his email address had been inundated with requests to get me back. So too his mobile phone messaging service. He talked about the fact that since his arrival companies were eager to invest in the club and that the decision to accept sponsorship for the tannoy could have been handled better. Indeed, he also complimented me on making the job sound easy, which probably didn't help newcomers to be accepted.

The outcome was to offer me my old role back but to try to work with Kiss 101 who would continue to supply the music and retain Jasper on the pitch. All I asked was that Wayne came back too. I knew he'd been gutted to lose his role on the pitch and it was agreed that he could share duties with Jasper.

It wasn't long, however, before Kiss 101 was dispensed with altogether. The music they supplied had little appeal to the majority of fans. From my understanding, they'd also reneged on their deal to advertise the club. Jasper stuck around for the rest of the season but didn't come back after that, although I did see him at Wembley and the odd game. It was a shame really as Jasper was a nice bloke. The kids in the family stand used to like him but older fans saw him as part of Kiss 101 and pulled his leg relentlessly, often calling him Norman Collier because his microphone kept cutting out.

Once again, it was back to Wayne and me, a Cardiff boy and a Valleys boy. As it should be! After all, our pairing was a fair reflection of our fan base.

CHAPTER 16

It wasn't long after the defeat to Russia that the FAW replaced Mark Hughes with his arch nemesis, John Toshack, a man who was openly critical of Hughes' tactics in the Welsh media, and with Tosh came a completely different approach. One of the changes included keeping everything low-key at Welsh internationals.

Speaking honestly, I was taken aback by the idea of low-key games at the Millennium Stadium. After all, one of the strengths of the stadium was its galvanising effect on the Welsh public, certainly for rugby games but also for football matches. For starters, there wasn't a bad seat in the place and, given the right encouragement, football fans were happy to get behind the team, sometimes making the stadium a formidable arena for visiting teams. Indeed, most footballers and managers talk about the supporters having the ability of being a twelfth man in the side and quite frankly, the Wales team needed all the help it could get, especially after half the team, the older, experienced members of the squad had called it a day after losing out on a place in the World Cup finals.

I have to say that I'd heard a lot about John Toshack, in particular his forthright and often spiky manner. I suppose if I'm honest though, I had mixed feelings about him, mostly negative, especially after he took Swansea into the First Division. I don't know why, but it felt like a betrayal from one of our own, I mean, a Cardiff boy, and local hero to boot, leading a fierce rival to the promised land, football's top table. It conjured up the same sort of feelings and emotions as when former favourites score against the Bluebirds. At the time, I hated it. It just wasn't right. That Swansea team of the 1980s could and should have been us. On top of that, I always had the impression from Tosh that he had a real grudge against his hometown for spurning his desire to manage the Bluebirds.

Anyway, a training session at the Millennium Stadium gave me the opportunity to introduce myself and judge the man for myself. Unfortunately, he was exactly how others had described him, a cantankerous, grumpy old man whose ego knew no bounds. I remember thinking what is it with some in football? It's not as if they've ever split the atom or taken part in groundbreaking brain surgery or rocket science. They've just learned to kick a ball or, in Tosh's case, to put his head to it. For me, football has never been a science and, as much as I enjoy it, it's still just a game.

Anyway, on asking him what he meant by 'low-key' matches, his answer was simple and blunt. "Just do the exact opposite of what you did when Mark Hughes was in charge. Keep it simple. I don't even want them cheering when we score," he blurted. As he walked away, I looked at the former Liverpool boss, Roy Evans, who had been standing next to him. He laughed and told me to ignore Tosh and carry on as normal.

Despite Roy Evans' reassuring words however, out went the pre-match bands and half-time entertainment from the usual itinerary, and in came… well, absolutely nothing. Indeed, such was Tosh's insistence on keeping things simple on and off the field that, along with a number of defeats, most of the passion at Welsh internationals disappeared from home games overnight. Tosh also wanted to take some of the games away from Cardiff, not to Wrexham but out west, reinforcing my view that his affinity to Swansea was greater than that towards his place of birth.

I guess that was the beginning of the end for me with the FAW. That and the deal they'd signed with Sky TV to televise live games. I say Sky TV because of a spat I had with one of their production managers and the subsequent action taken by the FAW after some pretty vindictive and underhanded tactics employed by the person in question. Bizarrely, I never got to know the fellow's name.

Having worked in television for the best part of twenty-five years, I can say with some confidence that production managers are breeds unto themselves. In fairness, over the years I've worked with some of the best. However, I've also come across some of the worst too. These tend to be the kind of bullies most people despise – blokes who model themselves on old-style nightclub bouncers, and most probably would have been had they not had a big break and got themselves into television companies. In fact, as a producer/director in television myself, I have had more than my fair share of run-ins with these types of production managers.

Prior to the gates opening, our usual pre-match routine was to sound check any musicians and singers, whether they be part of the build-up to games or there for the performance of the anthems. And, because of the nature of the Millennium Stadium, it was necessary to have floor speakers dotted around the stadium with a mixer situated on a desk behind the Wales team bench. However, it was always abundantly clear which Sky TV production manager was on duty by the respect afforded the PA lads whose desk I shared. The better production managers co-operated fully and we, in turn, did our best to accommodate them too: whether they needed a bit of space or the PA turned down so that the presenters could do their introductions, pieces to camera or conduct interviews on the pitch. Also, having spent a great many years working alongside them on a variety of television productions, particularly on dramas, most of the Sky technicians at the stadium were friends of mine. In fact, most were Welsh and had the same attitudes towards production managers as myself, borne out by the years of negotiating fees and conditions.

This particular production manager had long been a foe of mine and he had little regard for the FAW. Indeed, his demeanour at Welsh internationals was that it was an inconvenience to him, and merely a stepping stone to being awarded an England fixture. Whenever he was working for Sky TV, our desk was taken over by the television broadcaster. Indeed, he did everything to hamper the smooth running of the event from the FAW's perspective, causing mayhem to the sound check schedule and trying his best to make the FAW look unprofessional. He was also none to pleased with the positive relationship I had with his own television crew which, for some reason, he took as a slight. I guess respect brings respect; however, he was obviously of the opinion that life had a pecking order and, in his own mind, he was somewhere near the top whilst the Welsh were definitely below him.

After half a dozen games over the course of two years,

things came to a head. Strangely enough, whenever he'd caused a problem in the past, a quick phone call to the FAW chief, David Collins, soon resolved matters and the production manager would be reminded that the fixture said 'Wales versus' and not 'Sky TV versus'. Unbeknown to me, however, he was about to move jobs within Sky TV and after backing down so often, he wanted to make one last point. Well, for his last Welsh international, he pulled out all the stops, so much so that the Sky TV technicians warned me that the guy was on the warpath.

It didn't take him long to start his shenanigans and with it, wind me up. His first step was to get the technicians to cover the FAW desk with Sky equipment. He then told a bemused PA crew that they would not be able to set up in their usual spot as Sky had to use all available desk space. And finally, he'd instructed the anthem singer and band that they wouldn't be able to sound check because he needed silence for any possible interviews for their live broadcasts, despite the fact that this was two hours or more before kick-off and that there was actually nobody around to interview nor were there cameras, or cameraman for that matter, in place to film these bogus interviews.

Suffice to say, and as most who know me would confirm, I'm certainly no shrinking violet in the face of adversity or bullies. I removed the equipment myself and told the PA lads to set up. Word soon got to the production manager and a few minutes later out he came in a state of rage. He marched up to the desk and ordered the PA lads to remove their equipment again and replace it with Sky's equipment – monitors and microphones, etc. He also tried his best to embarrass me with a few choice put-downs. I guess he hadn't done his homework on me and soon found himself on the receiving end of a verbal hammering. Without going into too much detail, let's just say that I told him in no uncertain terms what I thought of him and his methods.

Before too long the argument between us was starting to draw a crowd, mainly of Sky technicians and stadium stewards. However, as he tried ordering them back to work, they stood stock-still. In fact, one remarked, "No, this is much more fun." "What is?" he spat out. "Watching Ali put you in your place!" came the reply.

Following the jeers of his own staff, he stomped off. He returned a short while later with Gerry Toms, the new Millennium Stadium manager, and accused me of abusing him. Gerry calmed the situation and that, I thought, was that. After all, as far as Gerry was concerned, it was one person's word against another.

Nevertheless, despite Gerry's intervention, the production manager came back a few minutes later and told me that our spat wasn't over. A shocked Half-time Wayne, who'd joined me for a coffee by then, asked him if he was threatening me. Of course, that was exactly what he was doing, although not in a physical way. He was too much of a coward for that.

A week or so later I was summoned to see David Collins at the FAW's headquarters. In his hand was a letter from Sky TV's legal department accusing me of threatening behaviour. Despite my protestations, David felt that the relationship with Sky TV was too important to jeopardise and told me that the FAW were no longer going to use my services on the tannoy. I was gutted.

The Sky TV crew have since covered a lot of Cardiff City games and I have a great working relationship with their regular production managers. Also, after a break of three years, I've resumed working for the FAW on the tannoy again, but only when the games have taken place at the Cardiff City Stadium.

As for the Millennium Stadium, the FAW now employ an English company and pay a considerable amount to provide the same service I did for next to nothing. In saying that, I have nothing against others working on the tannoy, everyone has their time. That said, I still get a lot of people asking me why I no longer do the international games at the Millennium Stadium, and that the present incumbents aren't as good, which is always nice to hear.

CHAPTER 17

The year 2008 will always be remembered for one thing. It was the year that Cardiff City reached the FA Cup final for the third time in the club's history. Of course, like all Cardiff fans, I have many fond memories of the campaign. However, if I was pinned down to picking three, I'd say that they would have to be an invite to join the Middlesbrough announcer in his box for our quarter-final match at the Riverside Stadium, along with both the semi-final and final appearances at Wembley.

I had telephoned the Boro announcer, Mark Page, to tell him that I was coming to the game and he kindly arranged for me to watch him at work. In all honesty, as much as I love Cardiff City, I'd never travelled that far before to support the team. The furthest north I'd been had been to Oldham back in the 1980s and, despite several attempts to persuade me, I had always declined going any further, especially when the only fixture further north was against the likes of Carlisle United, and usually in a midweek match or on a Friday night.

Anyway, this was different. It's not everyday you got to watch the club in an FA Cup quarter-final. I'd been gutted that I was on holiday in Egypt the last time we'd played Boro in the FA Cup. That was when we beat them 2–1 in a replay at Ayresome Park in 1994. In fact, I'd listened to the first game on the BBC's World Service in Alexandria and still remember the shocked expressions of family members in Egypt as I ran around the room in excitement after Garry

Thompson had equalised to make the score 2–2. I'd even tried to book an early flight home, but to no avail, much to my mother's disbelief. Whatever, this was a fixture I looked forward to, even if it meant over six hours on a coach just to get there. Three thousand other Cardiff fans had made the journey and Mark was the perfect host. He welcomed me and gave me an impromptu tour of the stadium before taking me to his box situated, strangely enough, in the away end.

Mark's duties included doing a stint on the pitch pre-match and at half-time. There was no clear way of reaching the pitch from his position at the back of the stand. Indeed, the easiest way of getting there was to walk through the away fans and, although he'd never met Cardiff fans before, he assured me that he'd made the trip many times and was well used to having banter with visiting fans. However, each time Mark attempted to reach the pitch, he disappeared into a throng of over-excited and slightly drunk Cardiff fans and was inadvertantly bashed several times on the back of his head by a giant papier-mâché daffodil that had made its way from south Wales. In fact, such was the size of the daffodil and the drunken over-exuberant nature of the lads holding it, that bits of debris from the daffodil clung to Mark's hair and clothing every time he passed it.

The Boro game has to go down as one of my all-time favourite away games. The 3,000 City fans in the Riverside Stadium contained faces I'd grown up with on the terraces of Ninian Park – people that I'd no idea as to what their names were but felt as one with them nonetheless. Having had a pitch-side pass from Mark, I remember clambering over the small fencing after winning the game, much to the shock of the Boro stewards, and legging it over to the players to congratulate them. Unbeknown to me at the time, several of the Boro stewards had started to chase me before being reassured by Cardiff stewards that I worked for the club. Back with the fans, the buzz outside the ground was incredible. Complete strangers hugged and kissed each other. Indeed, I saw one even trying to kiss a police horse. The trip was made all the more memorable by seeing the Boro fans clapping our buses as we left Teesside. I've always had a soft spot for Boro fans since then.

The semi-final was equally as memorable. Not only was it my first-ever trip to Wembley, but I'd also been invited by the FA to do a stint on the tannoy before kick-off.

I'd been told to get to Wembley early enough for a sound check, well before the gates opened and managed to get a lift there with Peter, Cardiff's official photographer. Surprisingly, rather than meeting many Cardiff fans en route, when we stopped at a service station on the M4 we were confronted by a few thousand Ospreys fans heading in the same direction for an important rugby fixture. I guess most of them had decided to leave early rather than share the facilities with Cardiff City fans that were likely to number tens of thousands.

I love the Millennium Stadium but, particularly for football fans, Wembley has a special aura all of its own. Also, considering, like thousands of other Cardiff fans, that I'd spent most of my time supporting the club as it yo-yoed between the lower leagues, getting to watch them in the home of football was something I'd never thought would happen in my lifetime. And now, not only was that dream about to be fulfilled, I was also going to get to speak Welsh on its tannoy, the first time that anyone had been allowed to do so. In fact, looking back, I'd probably have got away with saying anything in Welsh as none of the FA would have been any the wiser.

The lads operating the tannoy at Wembley worked for a company called Event 360, a company I was familiar with, having worked with them on several occasions at the Millennium Stadium. Event 360 covered a number of high-profile football games, from the FA Cup and League Cup finals to English and Welsh internationals. Their schedules tend to be pretty exact, with little room for manoeuvre. In other words, if you missed your allotted slot or said something untoward, they were quick to let you know about it. In fact, both the Barnsley announcer and I had been given five minutes each in total, which would include a club song or anthem. Therefore, if we ran over in terms of speaking, the club anthem would get faded out early. No pressure then!

I have to say that the Barnsley announcer, whose name escapes me, was a real gentleman. Like me, he'd been a fan of his local club from day one and, likewise, had never thought he'd ever see his team in an FA Cup semi-final, let alone at Wembley. After he'd done his stint, it was my turn. "Ladies and gentlemen, please welcome the Cardiff City announcer, Ali Yassine," boomed the Event 360 announcer. The response was incredible. Maybe it was something to do with just being happy to be there but, in hindsight, Cardiff fans on the whole, appeared to be much louder in the semi than in the final itself. The Barnsley announcer was equally as shocked by the roar. "Aye oop," he said as he handed me the microphone, "you're right popular, you are. Ain't ya!"

The funny thing is I have absolutely no recollection of what I said. It was almost like one of those outer-body experiences people talk about. I could hear myself speaking but it was as though the world had stopped for a few moments.

Incidentally, with regards to the club songs, after consultation, it was decided that the Beatles' 'Hey Jude' would be played as our anthem. However, it kind of bugged me that 'Hey Jude' was a song that lots of clubs claimed as their own. It certainly wasn't unique to Cardiff. Barnsley, on the other hand, had had some sort of dance track remixed especially for them. Thankfully, I'd taken a copy of 'Men of Harlech' with me just in case and, after seeing the Barnsley fans responding to their song, asked the tannoy boys to get rid of 'Hey Jude' and play 'Men of Harlech' instead.

Talk about inspired! Wembley had never heard its like before. If the Barnsley fans had been loud, the Cardiff fans were almost shaking the place to its foundations. I knew most would not know the words. I guess we all knew that. But it still made the hairs on the back of the neck stand up hearing over 30,000 Cardiff fans roaring their approval to it.

The tannoy boys kindly let me sit with them to watch the game, along with Darcy Blake, who scoffed most of the free food laid on for us. In fact, it was probably one of the best seats in the place and meant that not only did we have a perfect view but we also had access to the tunnel and pitch-side. Indeed, walking around the side of the pitch with Half-time Wayne and Bartley, the mascot, was such a buzz, doing the Ayatollah as Wayne took photos of the Cardiff fans for the club's website.

As for the small matter of the game itself, well, in spite of a wonder goal from Joe Ledley, it was no classic by any stretch of the imagination. Nobody cared though. The solitary goal that separated us meant that Cardiff City was going back to Wembley for the FA Cup final, in my case, minus one giant Welsh flag. Funnily enough, the flag in question appeared in all the papers the following day draped over Joe's shoulders. In fact, there's a cartoon caricature of Joe with the flag on the concourse at the Cardiff City Stadium. A giant flag with a picture of Joe holding it was made for the final and placed on Wembley's pitch. I had given it to him at the end of the match. However, when I asked for it back, he merely apologised and said that he'd thrown it into the fans. Thanks, Joe!

After announcing the final score the official announcer thrust the microphone in my hand and told me to have some fun. Caught off guard and with the match day programme in hand I did but, on a roll, I also decided to go through the squad to get our fans to cheer them all individually. Nothing untoward with that, I thought. That was, until I realised that some of the players I was announcing weren't even at the club any longer. The FA had made a balls-up of the squad list. Still, nothing was going to spoil this amazing day for me or the thousands of others celebrating wildly in Wembley.

As Peter, the photographer, and I walked back to the car park, we saw quite a few of Barnsley's celebrity fans trying to get to their cars as well. Some were trying their best, but to no avail. Michael Parkinson was one, a man much taller than I'd expected. He was taking Barnsley's loss in good spirits, even though he was stopped every few yards by autograph hunters, including dozens of Cardiff's pulling his leg over the win. One or two even tried impersonating him, badly. Not really a good idea, within punching distances of such a giant of a man, but he took it well.

We also saw the cricket umpire, Dickie Bird, and the former England bowler and now broadcaster, Darren Gough. They too were taking a ribbing from Cardiff fans, many shouting, "Howzat!" but both kept smiling. In fairness, Barnsley fans were a good bunch. You had to feel for them in a way as they'd seen their team on an incredible giant-killing run, knock out Liverpool at Anfield in the fifth round and Chelsea at their ground, Oakwell, in the quarter-final, only to come unstuck to a fellow Championship side, agonisingly close to an FA Cup final. Still, they'd got to see their team at Wembley, in a game that guaranteed a Championship club would be in the final. I was just grateful it was us.

CHAPTER 18

If the FA Cup semi-final had been a day to remember, then the final was certainly a day to forget, not because of the result but for a whole multitude of other reasons.

The media frenzy prior to the game had been an intense affair with broadcast and press media descending on the club in numbers never seen before, all looking for a particular angle. Even I got in on the act. My mobile phone seemed to ring continuously with requests for interviews from local and national press, and radio. I guess all the mad announcements that had made their way onto the BBC football website in their 'Quotes of the Week' section had gone before me with many looking for a sound bite.

It wasn't all positive press though. Some were questioning our right to represent the Football Association in Europe, while a certain Leighton James when asked for his view claimed that, as a Swansea fan, he would be supporting our opponents, Portsmouth, rather than a fellow Welsh team. In fact, James had written in his column for *South Wales Evening Post* that he would also like Cardiff City to lose to Barnsley FC in the semi-final, a view made all the more absurd considering his previous staunch attitude that Welsh people should always support Welsh teams in whatever sport, an opinion he had discussed at length on radio phone-in programmes.

In hindsight, the negativity and vitriol emanating from down the M4 in the build-up to the game should have been expected. At best, it was petty jealousy, and at worst, sheer contempt at all things Cardiff. I guess, out west, anything and everything that comes Cardiff's way is seen as a slight against Swansea. With regards to Cardiff's FA Cup run, accusations of an easy ride in the competition became common-place as well as a perceived notion of favoured treatment from the FAW to likely player suspensions that affected the capital's club. Of course, most Welsh clubs wished us well but I can't remember a single message of good luck from Swansea. Even Lee Trundle, a former Swansea striker, was keen to have a dig.

In the case of Leighton James and, indeed, Lee Trundle, I couldn't let them get away with their remarks and, at our final league game of the season, took the opportunity to pay them back with remarks of my own. As it happened, the game was against Barnsley.

At an opportune moment before kick-off, I turned on the microphone. "Ladies and gentlemen. We've had a letter from Leighton James." The packed Ninian Park began booing. "No, hear him out. Anyway, Leighton says that he's very, very sorry for the bad things he's said about Cardiff City, especially his comments before our game with Barnsley in the FA Cup and our upcoming game against Portsmouth in the final. He now hopes that we win the FA Cup for Wales. He's also requested that you stop sending the nasty mail. Also, could you please refrain from posting unpleasant bits of human waste through his letterbox. Furthermore, please stop sending the taxis, the emergency services and the takeaway food to his house at three o'clock in the morning. He has been inundated with pizzas and Indian and Chinese takeaways. Incidentally,

Lee Trundle has also been in touch and has asked that
you also stop sending the taxis and nasty mail to his house
but can you please, please, please keep the food coming!
Thank you."

All criticism aside, I loved the buzz around the city and
the football club before the FA Cup final. We'd won our
final game of the season against Barnsley, the result being
3–0, with a rather more convincing performance than the
semi had been. Also, I'd had a real laugh on the tannoy,
getting away with risqué songs and the odd announcement,
such as asking all and sundry to remain in the ground after
the match to thank the players for their efforts over the
course of the season, adding that they shouldn't bother
leaving early as we'd locked the gates. "There is no escape,
no escape!" I claimed, in my best dalek voice.

The procedure for the final was much the same as the
semi had been. I had been told to get to Wembley in good
time for a sound check. This time, however, I decided to
travel by coach with other supporters and on arrival was
introduced to my counterpart from Portsmouth, a chap
called Steve Pearson who wasn't just the club's announcer
but was their 'musicologist' as well. In essence, it meant
that he chose the match day music, which is hardly rocket
science. I guess it's like describing a toilet attendant as a
human waste-disposal engineer.

Anyway, Steve spent most of the pre-match build-up
telling all and sundry that he was the cousin of the former
Manchester Utd and West Ham player, Stuart Pearson,
and that his dad had played for Norwich in the 1940s and
1950s. Steve also wanted everyone to know that he was

the current Premier League Announcer of the Year. (Add your own fanfare here!)

To be honest, I didn't even know there was such an award. It did, however, beg the question as to why such an award existed. I mean, I could understand having a Player of the Year or a Manager of the Year but an Announcer of the Year! Thinking about it, what does an announcer have to do to win it? Was Steve Pearson the best reader of a team sheet in the division or possibly the season's most accomplished announcer of a birthday message? I later found out that it was because he'd played the most songs supplied by one of the many companies that put music together for football grounds. In other words, a particular company had rewarded him for plugging their music. One thing I'll say about music I receive in the post is that 99 per cent of it is utter garbage, often sent to football clubs because radio stations probably refuse to play the songs. Having spent years giving these CDs the benefit of the doubt, I don't even bother opening the padded envelopes anymore and either give them away or file them, usually in the bin. In fact, a more suitable title for Steve's award would have been 'Musical Prostitute of the Year' or the 'I'll Play Any Old Crap' award.

Anyway, after exchanging pleasantries, Steve's persona quickly shone threw. He quietly insisted that as he was with the 'Premier League' club, it was only right that he had the choice to go first or second when it came to turns on the microphone. To be honest, I wasn't bothered either way but, on checking the running order for the day, I'd seen that Steve was due to go first. On pointing this out to him, he declared that the running order was just a guide and could be adjusted. However, having worked with the organisers, Event 360, on a number of occasions, I knew that they liked sticking to their running orders like glue. Indeed, the running orders were subject to FA approval and were often only put together after a number of meetings with them. After all, it was their gig.

Despite this, Steve was having none of it. He wanted to go last and that was that. Unfortunately for him, that wasn't how Event 360 saw things and, after a few choice words, mostly swear words aimed in Steve's direction, he resigned himself to going on first, as scripted. If only that had been the end of it. Not so!

Earlier that morning, I'd been told that, as opposed to the semi, I wasn't allowed to speak Welsh this time around and that the FA had brought in a rule stating that no Welsh should be used over the tannoy whatsoever. Strangely, despite pointing out that the Welsh national anthem, 'Hen wlad fy nhadau', was being sung before kick-off by the classical singer, Katherine Jenkins, I was told that she was actually singing 'Land of my fathers'. Doh!

I watched Steve do his stint to mixed reviews and got prepared myself for my five minutes of fame. There seemed to be half as many Cardiff fans as Portsmouth fans in the stadium and, after a sharp intake of breath, I began. "Ladies and gentlemen, boys and girls, Cardiff City fans – let's be clear about today. We are not here just representing a football club. Nor are we here just representing the beautiful city of Cardiff. We are here representing an entire nation!" At this point, Steve saw red and interjected. "What do you think this is, pal? A political broadcast!" he bellowed. Unperturbed, I continued speaking. "Cardiff City fans, your nation needs you, your city needs you and your football club needs you! Do your duty! Support the boys and make some noise!" The cheers that emanated around the stadium seemed almost twice as loud as the Portsmouth fans had been and, as the music for 'Men of Harlech' began, Steve had had enough, losing complete control of his emotions. Grabbing a Pompey flag from the nearest person, he began waving it in my face. Aghast at his actions, the lads from Event 360 prodded him but to no avail. He continued waving the flag. However, as 'Men of Harlech' rang out, I put my hand in my coat pocket and pulled out the mother of Welsh flags. Indeed, having lost my last one in the semi, I'd bought another in the Ninian Park car park prior to leaving. It was twice the size of Steve's flag. I stood on a seat and held it towards the direction of the Cardiff fans. "Mine's bigger than yours!" I said smugly.

Prior to kick-off, my day was made all the more memorable by having a photo taken with Katherine Jenkins, however, that was as good as it got. Indeed, as with most Cup finals, the game was way too tense to enjoy. Also, Portsmouth had been nailed on to win it. We did have our moments though, including a disallowed goal. That said, Pompey were too strong and too determined.

When it was all over, as gutting as it was to lose, there was a definite sense of pride in being there, especially seeing all the Cardiff fans that had stayed behind to congratulate Portsmouth, something noted by the FA and the wider media. Furthermore, as Pompey continued their celebrations, I popped into the FA's office in the bowels of the stadium to say my goodbyes and was presented with a number of flags as a souvenir of my visit and Cardiff City's FA Cup campaign. Each had the FA's logo on them with the words 'Cardiff City' and 'Winners'.

CHAPTER 19

Like everyone else at the club, as much as I looked forward to moving to the new stadium rising from the ashes across the road, leaving Ninian Park was always going to be a hell of a wrench. Of course, the club needed to move on and the old ground had outlived its use, but it was where all my football-loving mates and I grew up in terms of following Cardiff City, and it held many fond memories.

Happy memories aside, the last game at Ninian Park, a league game against Ipswich, encapsulated the ups and downs of following Cardiff City. Once again, just when hope had overcome adversity, just when we dared dream that we could be promoted to the country's Premier League, needing just a point to more or less secure a play-off position, the team succumbed to lower opposition, losing emphatically in the process. Ninian Park deserved a better sending off than that 3–0 defeat, yet the result summed up perfectly my time as a Bluebird fan.

Worse still was the so-called celebration on the pitch to mark the end of the era, with 'cheap' written all over it. From the cheap flame throwers hired for the day to the cheap plastic balls kicked onto the terraces by the players. So cheap were the balls, in fact, that many didn't make it that far; the wind almost repelling the very idea of treating the stadium with such little respect. It was an event easily forgotten.

On the other hand, some things will always stay in the memory. For me, as I've mentioned elsewhere in the book, it's often been the bizarre events that are associated with games rather than the games themselves. One of these took place when tickets became available for an FA Cup game against Manchester City in 1994, a game that had all the drama a City fan could ever want – from an exquisite goal scored by Nathan Blake to an amazing penalty save by Mark Grew. And, of course, the incredible atmosphere generated within Ninian Park, helped no doubt by the 5,000 travelling Manchester City fans that day. However, as I said, I remember the game and Ninian Park for something altogether different.

I arrived early at Ninian Park with my regular Grange End mates, Mike and Jeremy, when the tickets went on sale. Despite our punctuality, thousands of others had beaten us to it – thousands we'd never seen at Ninian Park that season. Indeed, by the time we got to the stadium, the queue had snaked its way from the turnstiles in the Canton Stand, around the old Supporters' Club building, to the main road outside and had almost reached the Grange End some hundred yards away at the other end of the ground.

As we made our way to the back of the queue, I spotted a young mother with a toddler strapped in a pushchair trying desperately to get past the throng of people filling the pavement outside the ground. It had rained heavily the night before and, as she negotiated a number of huge puddles, an over eager fan barged his way past her trying to get to his mates. In doing so he kicked up water, which soaked the youngster in the pushchair, causing him to burst into tears. The culprit, a six foot four man in his thirties, looked back, tutted and walked away. I saw red, and followed and caught up with him, and asked why he hadn't apologised. At that he called his friends over and, surrounded by five or six men, it clicked that it may not have been a good idea to demand an apology. However, a number of others had seen his actions and joined me, including by then the friends I had gone with who had located me in the mêlée. The culprit and his friends soon backed away.

As luck would have it, we ended up a few yards behind this bunch and, as we queued, Mike made it his business to tell all and sundry about the incident, embarrassing the hell out of them. While this took place, I remembered that we had passed a hot dog kiosk near the Canton Stand and decided to leave the queue to seek out a cup of tea. Alas, the kiosk had run out of water but, as I trundled back to my friends, I bumped into another Grange End regular who had a mate keeping his place near the front of the queue. He told me to join him and within a matter of minutes I was holding four tickets.

By the time I'd returned to my friends, Mike was in overdrive. In fact, I was beginning to feel sorry for the water-splasher and his mates who were taking a right verbal pounding. Mike, on the other hand, was in his element and saw no reason for respite. I suppose his madcap sense of humour was one of the reasons we'd become friends. He really was off the wall, so to speak. More than anything, he loved an audience and fed off the laughter emanating from his jibes. The objects of his fun, however, were beginning to feel more than a bit agitated by the attention. Seeing that they were getting more and more fed up with the digs at them, Mike decided to change tack, faking sincerity whilst asking what they thought of the team that season. His victims looked at each other, unsure of how to respond.

During this respite I took the opportunity to show Mike that I'd bought our tickets already. He took them from me, winked and marched up to the lads in front, waving the tickets at them.

"Look, lads, I'm sorry for taking the piss out of you. I was only having a laugh."

"It's OK, no harm done."

"Tell you what. Do you want to buy some tickets? We've got a few spares."

"Yes, please. How much do you want for them?"

"Oh, bugger! I just remembered. Sorry, I can't sell them to you."

"Why not?"

"Because you're a bunch of twats!" he replied.

Another incident I remember well was in 1998 when Wales took on Jamaica in an international friendly. I'd seen Wales play several times at Ninian Park. Some of these included European Championship games and the Home Nations tournament, including one match when Cardiff's Phil 'Joe' Dwyer scored against England. However, the reason I remember the Jamaica match so well is because of two Jamaican fans that stood next to Jeremy and me.

At the time, I was playing guitar in a reggae band, so was made up to hear reggae played over the tannoy as we entered the ground. The other sense stirred by the match was my sense of smell. Despite being in the open, the air was thick with the unmistakable, yet pungent smell of cannabis. In fact, so much of it was being smoked in the ground that the police had obviously given up all hope of stopping it. It seemed a free for all.

As we took our place on the Bob Bank where the Welsh fans were supposedly placed, it was immediately obvious that Jamaica fans had no respect for crowd segregation, almost filling half the stand. To be honest though, I loved it. I'd never seen so many black people at Ninian Park. Talk about feeling right at home. Nevertheless, it soon became apparent that these were not the kind of people I'd grown up with in the Docks area of Cardiff. For one thing, I could barely understand a word they were saying. The patois emanating from their mouths was so thick that it was really difficult to make out any words. And this, from someone who prided himself on understanding even the broadest of Jamaican accents, due to a wide and varied collection of reggae albums. However, despite my record collection and boasting a number of friends with Caribbean roots, understanding the vocabulary of the visiting supporters was challenging to say the least.

Anyway, standing next to Jeremy and me were two lads of roughly the same age as us. Both had huge joints in their hands and were obviously revelling in the fact that they could smoke cannabis without fear of arrest. It was also obvious, with minutes to go before kick-off, that they were quite stoned, dancing away to the reggae emanating from the tannoy speaker above them. Being the friendly type I tried to engage them in conversation:

"Alright, lads!"

"Wa gwan, bwoy!" ("What's happening, boy!")

"What's this Jamaica team like?"

"Dey is cris, mon! No one cyaan test dem." ("Yes, they are cool, man! No-one can compete with them.")

"Who's playing for them tonight, anyone we might know?"

"Yeah, dread!" ("Yes, dreadlocked person!")

"Who?"

"Naa worry bout it! Tan deh!" ("Don't worry about it! Just wait and see!")

"Do you know any of the team for tonight yet?"

"Yeah, mon. Big up uno dem!" ("Yes, man, praise them all!")

"Who's the main men then?"

"All a dem me bredren!" ("All of them are my brothers!")

"You reckon they'll win tonight, do you?"

"Wah wid all dese kwestions, bwoy?" ("What's with all these questions, boy?")

"I'm only asking. Just being friendly."

"Wah! Is you a batty bwoy?" (What! Are you gay?")

"What's that supposed to mean?"

"Naa mek mi vex, mon. Galang bout yuh business! Lef mi Nuh!" ("Don't make me angry, man. Go away! Leave me alone!")

As I turned to a by now laughing Jeremy, they continued their dancing and smoking. However, it was at the end of a dull 0–0 draw that things took the most comical of turns.

Still smarting from the put-down, I had largely ignored the Jamaican lads. Indeed, having seen them head for the refreshment kiosks during the half-time break without returning, I'd presumed that they'd either moved to another part of the Bob Bank or had had enough and had left the ground altogether. Much to my surprise, as the game came to a conclusion, one of them tapped my shoulder.

"Hey dread, wh'appen!" ("Hey dreadlocked person, what is happening!")

"Alright."

"Weh cyaan a bredda go?" (Where can a brother go?")

"Sorry?"

"Weh cyaan a bredda go an g'yet som akshun?" ("Where can a brother go for a good time?")

Coming from a person that had accused me of being gay, I was more than a little shocked by his question. If the truth be known, I was also more than a little confused by what he meant by the word 'action' and just stared at him open-mouthed. At this point, probably thinking my confusion stemmed from his dialect, the lad switched from Jamaican patois to a really thick Birmingham accent.

"D'yow know if there's a night cloob neer 'ere, mate?"

CHAPTER 20

If the last game at Ninian Park had ended in a whimper on the field of play, the first game at the Cardiff City Stadium started with an almighty bang. Indeed, the disappointment of missing out on a Championship play-off place by a solitary goal to Preston the previous season had cast a dark gloom over the summer months. However, a 4–0 thumping of Scunthorpe in our first competitive match at the Cardiff City Stadium soon changed the mood, giving us all renewed optimism for a promotion push in our first season at our new home, a stadium cruelly labelled, 'Legoland', for the colourful cladding that adorned its exterior.

For me, the new stadium was a tannoy announcer's dream. Mind you, anything was going to be better than the shed that I'd called home for so many years at Ninian Park, a PA room that was akin to being in a freezer during the winter and a sauna in the summer.

Prior to the building work commencing on the new stadium, I'd been consulted with regards to the tannoy room and offered a chance to have an input into its layout and design. In fact, a lot of other announcers, particularly those who have since visited the stadium, look on in envy because, as well as all the mod cons i.e. widescreen television, computers, etc., I have a prime position with a clear view of the pitch and a window that can be opened, enabling me to hear the tannoy and the fans singing and chanting first hand, as well as giving me access to instant fresh air. As strange as it sounds, my counterpart at Arsenal still can't believe that, despite spending many more millions on the Emirates Stadium than we did on our stadium, his facilities are nowhere near as good as mine. Also, the only way he can gauge the sound quality and level is by asking a steward with a walkie-talkie sat pitch-side. In fact, he spends most of his time completely unaware of how he sounds to the 60,000 plus who attend Arsenal's home matches. So much for progress! Furthermore, the Cardiff City Stadium boasted a kitchen a few feet from the PA room and a toilet within easy reach. No more crossing my legs, willing the referee to blow for half-time and inevitably racing to the nearest toilet and back, which was like attempting an assault course, barging past all and sundry in my attempt to get back to the tannoy before a particular song had finished on the CD player.

Anyway, as I intimated at the beginning of this chapter, the early form of the team gave many hope for a successful season. I suppose we all knew that, of the other teams, Newcastle and West Brom having been relegated from the Premier League, would be favourites for promotion. That said, it would be an even fight for the third spot on offer, and by Christmas the table confirmed this. As well as Nottingham Forest, who were six points ahead of us, Cardiff, Leicester and Swansea all sat tied on 37 points each.

The play-offs, of course, are a horrible experience, especially for fans and, having endured a defeat to Stoke and a win against Bristol City, Cardiff fans were well-versed in the ups and downs, the emotional rollercoaster that play-off matches brought with them.

As it turned out, we were to face Blackpool in our third game at Wembley in three years, a game that came about because of Blackpool's late run of good form in the league and subsequent demolition of Nottingham Forest in a play-off semi-final, coupled with our penalty win over Leicester in the other semi-final, thanks largely to Leicester's Yann Kermorgant who tried to score by chipping the Bluebirds' goalkeeper, David Marshall, but failed miserably. Indeed, it was one of those goals that would have given Kermorgant legendary status at Leicester, had he scored. As it was, it labelled him a chump and is remembered by Leicester fans as the £90 million penalty miss, which soon led to his departure from the club.

As with previous Wembley appearances, I was invited, along with my counterpart from Blackpool, to do a spot on the microphone pre-match to help create a bit of banter. This time around we were asked to speak from the centre circle as opposed to the tannoy position on the side of the pitch. Without monitors, hearing the speakers was impossible, the sound swirling about the place creating an echo effect. Indeed, having to wait about ten yards away from the Blackpool announcer and despite my best attempts to lip-read, I had no idea what was he was saying. When it came to my turn, the response seemed lukewarm, OK at best, but certainly nothing near as good as it had been during that first visit in the FA Cup semi-final. I guess back then had been more of an occasion to most of the fans that had made the trip. It was our first glimpse of the new Wembley and, despite the prestige, there wasn't £90 million resting on the game or the chance to visit places like Old Trafford, Anfield and Stamford Bridge.

I shook hands with the Blackpool announcer and headed for the tannoy booth. However, as we reached the side of the pitch, it became abundantly clear that all was not right. In fact, the reception we both had from the technicians couldn't have contrasted more. I was greeted with smiles and handshakes, he was stonewalled. It was only later that I heard that he had used his opportunity for banter to have a go at all of Blackpool's local rivals, Preston in particular, and thanked Nottingham Forest for letting Blackpool walk all over them. Paul, the Arsenal and England announcer and the main announcer for the day, turned to me and declared, "Now, I'm definitely supporting Cardiff today!"

Unfortunately, it wasn't to be our day and despite taking the lead twice, Blackpool just never gave up the fight. The guts they displayed that day was something we all admired, their fans and ours alike and, if I was being honest, I'd wished we'd had their desire. It wasn't meant to be, and Cardiff City were quickly earning the label of 'the nearly men'. We'd nearly won the FA Cup, we'd nearly made the play-offs and we'd nearly got promoted.

A lot of fans remember the awful feeling of losing to Stoke in a play-off semi-final but nothing comes close to the emotions felt after losing a final. I'll never forget leaving Wembley that day. The journey home seemed to take an age. In fact, getting away from the stadium took forever itself with the agony of defeat made worse by the joy of the Blackpool fans waving their flags and dancing in jubilation, many of them there to watch their local team for the first time. On top of that, the agony was prolonged by the radio stations revelling in their victory, drooling over 'little Blackpool' sitting at football's top table. Getting home couldn't come soon enough. I didn't want to watch another football match for as long as I lived and certainly had no desire to pick the meat from the bones of the game. How ironic then that after plonking myself on the sofa at home and turning on the television, on came the BBC Wales' highlights programme. I couldn't watch. In fact, I still can't watch. Too many bad memories, I guess.

CHAPTER 21

Nobody likes hearing negative feedback, me included, however, whenever I get negative feedback, I often hear the words "welcome to our world" by full-time members of staff. What they mean, I suppose, is that their week is sometimes wholly dependent on the team's performance. If the team does well, the reaction of most fans they come into contact with is a positive one. However, when the team plays badly, everyone gets it in the neck, whether it's through face-to-face contact, on the phone or on football messageboards.

I guess the people most likely to take abuse from fans are those working in the ticket office, the club shop staff and the receptionists. In other words, the staff working on the frontline. And they often get blamed for everything.

In my case, the complaints I've received over the years have been varied, ranging from an irate vicar complaining about my desecration of the Lord's Prayer to an upset parent that hadn't heard his child's birthday request, and from a livid Chief Executive (Peter Ridsdale) unhappy that I'd played a song about fat girls, to a follically-challenged football fan none too pleased about a quip I'd made about bald people.

Despite its popularity among a large section of the supporters, some complain about my pre-match tag line 'Support the boys and make some noise', a tag line I borrowed from my counterpart at Reading, Paul Allen, some ten years ago. Paul started at around the same time as me and has since told me that he had borrowed it from someone else.

Along with Reading's equivalent of Half-time Wayne – a chap called Stuart, Paul was a guest in the PA room at the Cardiff City Stadium for the Championship play-off semi-final second leg between the Bluebirds and the Royals, and was taken aback by the amount of people that joined in every time I shouted it over the tannoy. Indeed thanks to his Twitter account, it's now on the internet.

In recent times I've also received criticism for trying to get all four sides of the stadium singing in unison. It occurred to a few of the staff that many of the newer fans didn't know the older songs that used to emanate from the Ninian Park terraces. I guess with a new stadium comes increased interest from a new generation of Cardiff fans – fans that were probably reluctant to come in the past because of a perceived negative reputation, especially when it came to bringing their children too. To resolve the matter, it was suggested that I acted as an impromptu cheerleader. In fairness, hearing so many people singing in unison made the hairs on the back of the neck stand up. In fact, in a televised game against QPR, the BBC commentators commended the support for being so passionate. The feedback was excellent. However, when the same tactics were employed a week later with a similar pre-match response from the supporters but, alas, the team lost, it was an opportunity for some to lay the blame on my shoulders. As the full-time staff had pointed out, "welcome to our world".

The recurring themes with regards to complaints about the tannoy, however, seem to be over the choice of music and the use of Welsh.

Music is, of course, subjective. Everyone has their own preferences and, over the course of the last ten years or so, I've tried my best to accommodate most tastes, from jazz-funk to thrash metal and from ska punk to truck-driving country trip hop. At some point or other during the average season, most styles get an airing and, depending on the demand, some more than once, particularly chart music. Yet, no matter what I play, the complaints still keep coming. It's either too much of one thing or not enough of another. Some are keen to hear music when a goal is scored – others shudder at the thought of 'americanising' football. Some want to choose a classic rock track for the team to enter the pitch to, others want to pick a piece of classical music. Some want the volume loud to build up an atmosphere, others think there should be no music, so that the fans can create an atmosphere by themselves with no encouragement from the tannoy or, indeed, don't care about creating an atmosphere at all and want the music low enough to allow them to chat to their friends. There's simply no way you can please everybody and I have long stopped trying. However, my motto with regard to the music is that I can please some of the people some of the time but there's no way I can please all of the people all of the time. In saying that, almost all of the music played over the tannoy has been requested at some point or other. In fact, I sometimes think that the best way of resolving musical differences is to have a giant jukebox located somewhere in the ground, where fans can pop a pound into a slot and choose a song of their choice.

Another area of complaint is the use of the Welsh language on the tannoy. As it happens, Welsh tannoy announcements are now part of the club's commitment to the language. We have bilingual signs all over the exterior and interior of Cardiff City Stadium and we have a number of Welsh-speaking staff in various departments within the football club. We've also held Welsh lessons in the stadium and regularly hold conferences where the language is prevalent. However, for some reason, there are a minority of supporters that have a real issue with the language. Bizarrely, from my perspective, I actually speak very little Welsh on the tannoy other than welcoming fans to the stadium and when announcing the amount of time added on at the end of each half, plus the odd birthday greeting at half-time, obviously to a Welsh-speaker. I also try to play the odd Welsh-language song from time to time. Yet the use of a single word of Welsh seems to stir some into all manner of abuse, whether by means of a phone call to the club, in a letter or on the internet, often claiming that the Welsh language is irrelevant and has nothing to do with football or Cardiff City FC. Of course, the vast majority of people support the use of Welsh. After all, our club represents the capital city of Wales, so it's only right that the Welsh language is heard at Cardiff City games. It's also something that has the full support of away fans. Many of them have responded positively to the club reinforcing its Welsh identity, making their visits a bit more interesting and giving them the opportunity to sing their England songs and create a bit of friendly banter.

I can understand some of the reasons as to why there is a bit of animosity towards the language. However, most of it, in my humble opinion, is completely misplaced.

My first experience of hearing Welsh was as a youngster

born and brought up in Cardiff. This was before the days of S4C when Welsh-language programmes were dotted around the television schedules. I'll never forget watching Saturday morning programmes like *Bilidowcar* and *Teliffant* on the BBC as I waited for the English-language service to begin. I also remember helping out at Cardiff Arms Park in the early 1970s, usually getting there early on international days to take the plastic covers off the pitch, and was rewarded with free entry to the terraces. It was there that my Docks mates and me heard people communicate in the language for the first time and sing the national anthem. Not that we had a clue as to what it meant.

Later in life, I came to think that most Welsh speakers in Cardiff had the best of everything and to a certain extent this was true. Most lived in areas like Pontcanna or Llandaf and held jobs at the BBC. However, after learning the language in my twenties and spending a few years in the Welsh-speaking heartland of north Wales, my attitude toward Welsh speakers changed completely. In fact, I can honestly say that I have yet to meet a group of people that are more welcoming than north Walians, especially when you make an effort to speak their language. Wherever I went I was made to feel as Welsh as they were. Our differences in colour, culture and religion mattered not. We were part of the same family.

In saying that, there are a couple of instances where my own prejudices were put to the test. One of these was when I first arrived in Caernarfon and kept hearing the locals talking about a black boy, sometimes in front of me. Of course, this shocked me. My Welsh wasn't good enough to challenge them over it but I still felt none too pleased by their lack of respect. This went on for some weeks and I was getting angrier every time I heard the slur, to the point of almost losing my temper over it. One day, however, on a lunchtime walk through the town, I took a wrong turning and was briefly lost in some narrow streets leading off the main town centre. After asking for directions back to the local square and hearing the words 'black boy' again, I looked at the old man trying to help me in disgust. "Who are you calling a black boy?" I spat out. Quickly realising that I'd got the wrong end of the stick, he pointed to a sign further along the lane. "Not you!" he said. "That!" I looked towards the direction he was pointing. The Black Boy was the name of a pub, one of the oldest in Caernarfon. With a mixture of relief and embarrassment, I thanked him and quickly walked away.

Another time, in Bethesda, I was in a local pub playing pool. I wasn't a bad pool player at the time and, after a while, had pretty much beaten everyone in the pub. This was until one of the better local players turned up for his lunch. No matter how many times I tried, as soon as I passed the pool cue to him, in between munching a sandwich and sipping on his pint, that was end of sports. He'd clear the table more or less every time. Building up a bit of courage to use the little Welsh I had at the time, I asked him if he ever lost. He pointed to the trophies behind the bar and declared that he was the pub's team captain. One of the lads sitting near the table confirmed that nobody ever beat him, and certainly not on his 'home' table. He knew every nook and cranny of it. As the penny dropped, I laughed. The captain laughed too and said, "We don't get many like you in here." I looked at him in shock. "What? Black people who speak Welsh!" I exclaimed. "Don't be daft," he said, "people from Cardiff who speak Welsh." I didn't know where to look.

After over two decades of travelling back and forth to north Wales, I now consider the place like a second home. It's home to many friends – friends that have helped nurture my Welsh-language skills and have witnessed my fluency improve year on year.

I try to visit at least once a year, sometimes taking my children with me, who have also fallen in love with the people and places I hold so dearly. I've also been to north Wales with Cardiff City fans on a sponsored walk to the top of Snowdon and, along with Sam Hammam, most were taken aback by the welcome afforded me by the locals, whether by getting a reduced rate for parking on account of speaking Welsh or the warmth that comes with familiarity. One of the City fans remarked, "Bloody hell! Ali is like a local celebrity round here!"

I get the same welcome in west Wales. Indeed, Wales has some of the prettiest places and most welcoming people on earth, and it never ceases to amaze me that there are many people in south Wales who pay a fortune to go to places like the Pyrenees or the Alps every year, yet have never travelled around their own country. For me, the welcome I have received and continue to receive every time I travel around the country will always drive my desire to hear more Welsh in Cardiff and promote the oldest living language in Europe at the Cardiff City Stadium. As the last line of the anthem says, 'Long may the old language live on'.

Ironically, not one complaint has ever come in with regard to the use of the Malay language on the tannoy as a way of showing respect to our Malaysian owners and their match day guests. It's a funny old world!

CHAPTER 22

I would have loved to have begun this final chapter by declaring how jubilant I felt after finally seeing Cardiff City reach the Premier League, however that is just not Cardiff City. Indeed, as I write this final chapter, news has just filtered through that the club has terminated Dave Jones' contract after another season that promised so much but, in the end, delivered nothing.

There is no doubting that the football club has made great leaps during Dave Jones' time as manager, for a variety of reasons. We have a brand new stadium, a state-of-the-art training complex and have seen a calibre of player, that most of us could only dream of a few years ago, grace the pitch. We've also been to Wembley three times and have seen the team play at Anfield, Villa Park, Stamford Bridge and at the Emirates Stadium. That said, most Bluebirds fans agree that supporting Cardiff City has never been easy.

However, I guess the one thing that unites the majority of football fans, Man Utd apart, is that whichever team you support, particularly lower league clubs, sooner or later (usually sooner) they end up kicking you in the teeth. Worse still, you know it's going to happen, yet even when the writing is on the wall, somehow blind optimism still masks common sense and reasoning. And in my time as a Cardiff City fan, apart from a few odd exceptions, that's always been the case. We've always been the bridesmaid, never the bride. Some call it character building, citing that football teams merely reflect the ups and downs we all go through in life. Other, more astute individuals, particularly wives and girlfriends (no offence to female Cardiff fans) and my father, say that it's just a silly and irrational obsession.

Most of us accept that we can't all be successful – a little success would be nice – but we still keep going back for more, whatever the weather and whatever the circumstances. Even if it all gets too much for a while and we tear ourselves away from physically watching our team play, we still can't help seeking out the latest score, always in the vain hope that we taste just a little bit of success – such is the drug that football is. It's totally irrational, but football gives us something to look forward to, be you a youngster with a dream of playing it professionally, or an older cynic like myself that has learned to accept his lot in life.

The sad reality for most of us is, of course, failure, whether that's suffering the depressing experience of relegation, having our insides torn to shreds by missing out on promotion or getting knocked out of a Cup competition, sometimes in the cruellest of ways, as the team reaches its latter stages. Whatever, it always hurts.

In saying that, it's the misery of failure that makes any kind of success that bit sweeter, making up for all the heartache and broken dreams along the way. And there's no chance of switching allegiance to a more successful club, no matter how much admiration we may have for another team's success or style of play. Staunch Cardiff fan, Gwyn Davies, summed it up perfectly when he said, "I've had five wives, but just one football club!"

I guess as years go by, and as much as we hope for success, we find that there's so much more to being a fan of Cardiff

City than just the football. It's our sense of belonging to the club that is strengthened by familiarity. We belong to the same tribe. We sit in the same seat surrounded by the same people. We eat the same food and drink the same drink. We travel on the same route to the ground. We even wear the same 'lucky' shirt or socks or underwear.

As fans go, Cardiff City supporters range from the excited to the indifferent and from the dreamers to the realists. However, unlike the newer generation of Sky TV supporters, one thing is for certain, and that is that the vast majority of us have never been armchair supporters. The actor and Cardiff fan, Jonny Owen, once said that he was a Bluebirds fan because, collectively, we're not the type of people to boast our support for a club we live two hundred miles away from, only ever glimpsing our heroes on satellite television or on the rare visit to that team's stadium. I agree with him. What we feel is real. We're a part of it. Owners, managers, players, etc., have all come and gone but we're still there. We enjoy the few highs and suffer the all too often lows but just get on with it. I wouldn't trade any of that for anything. We agree and we disagree, and some even trade blows over it but we're never ordinary or placid. We give and we expect, sometimes too much.

As for working on the tannoy, that too has its highs and lows, its positives and negatives, but then so has every job. That said, I have yet to come across a job with so much emotion attached to it. If we win, a lot of fans think everyone and everything connected with the club is great. When we lose, everyone and everything is to blame, from the manager to the players, from the tea lady to the tannoy announcer. Furthermore, everything is analysed in great detail, whether that be the team selection, tactics or the price of a pint or pie. In my case, it never ceases to amaze me how every record, remark and intonation or inflection is picked upon and given extra meaning, intended or not, but then that's football.

I guess no matter how much I try, I know I'll never be everyone's cup of tea but I've learned to take the rough with the smooth. I never try to use the tannoy in a malicious way, no matter how tempting that is sometimes, but then again I've never been one to shrink into the background either. I guess I've made it my business to try to do something a little different. Some love it and want more, others hate it and wished that the club replaced me with a more sedate figure that simply read the team sheets and played a bit of background music. Again, that's football. As aficionados of the sport say, it's a game of opinions. However, opinions, as we all know, are like backsides. Everyone's got one!

Nevertheless, football has changes beyond recognition in the last ten years and so has the job of the humble tannoy announcer. With more money than ever, the sport has become more and more corporate. No longer can an announcer stamp the personality of the local support base on the tannoy or create a bit of banter between rival fans. Also, with more and more people within clubs, each with a grander job title than the last, demanding a greater input in what is broadcast over the airwaves and with each minute accounted for, fewer opportunities exist to give fans a laugh.

Announcers have changed too, with more and more sounding as though they've been cloned from the vast pool of safe DJs once the bastion of every local BBC radio station. Visits to grounds around the country appear to confirm that we have become a breed of nodding dogs, eager to please an owner or manager's every whim and too afraid to express an opinion in case it offends or loses us our jobs – a job we often care way too much about despite the pittance we're paid because we work for the club we love. We are now 'fun and engaging' as opposed to 'entertaining and edgy'. Slowly but surely, our personalities, much like the soul of football, are being ripped away from us.

Fans have changed too. The new generation of football supporter demands far greater success, quick to abandon a club after a bad season, indeed, some after a few defeats. Some even support multiple clubs, changing their allegiance from season to season or even from game to game.

I know one thing for sure. I'll never feel the same towards any other football club. For me, Cardiff City, as the song goes, is and will always be 'The greatest team in football the world has ever seen!'

'Was it Something I Said?' is just one of a whole range of publications from Y Lolfa. For a full list of books currently in print, send now for your free copy of our new full-colour catalogue. Or simply surf into our website

www.ylolfa.com

for secure on-line ordering.

TALYBONT CEREDIGION CYMRU SY24 5HE
e-mail ylolfa@ylolfa.com
website www.ylolfa.com
phone (01970) 832 304
fax 832 782